The Book of
BOOTY

The Book of BOOTY

Shake It Love It Never Be It

From WWE's The New Day

with Greg Adkins and Ryan Murphy

ST. MARTIN'S GRIFFIN
NEW YORK

Dedicated to Francesca I
2015-2016
The beat goes on.

Also dedicated to Francesca II
2016-2016
Please stop destroying
our trombones.

www.stmartins.com

The Library of Congress Cataloging-in-Publication Data Is Available upon Request

ISBN 9781250147004 (paper over board)
ISBN 9781250147011 (ebook)

Our books may be purchased in bulk for promotional, educational, or business use. Please contact your local bookseller or the Macmillan Corporate and Premium Sales Department at 1-800-221-7945, extension 5442, or by email at MacmillanSpecialMarkets@macmillan.com.

First Edition: March 2018

10 9 8 7 6 5 4 3 2 1

Design by studio2pt0, llc
Production by Stonesong

CONTENTS

Put on your virtual reality headset now for the full *Book of Booty* sensory experience*

*If your copy of *The Book of Booty* did not come with a virtual reality headset, you can make your own using some tinfoil, a salad bowl, and your granddaddy's reading glasses.

AROUND THE WORLD IN 483 DAYS

WWE Superstars Big E, Kofi Kingston, and Xavier Woods were on the verge of rewriting history.

The trio, known collectively as The New Day, had captured the prestigious WWE Tag Team Championships at *SummerSlam* on August 23, 2015. Now, if they could only retain those titles throughout the December 12, 2016, episode of *Monday Night Raw*, they would tie Demolition's 478-day run as the longest-reigning tag team champions in WWE history. Simple, right?

Not so fast. In *Raw*'s opening bout, the three-man thrill ride would find itself in the precarious position of having to defend the titles in a Triple Threat Tag Team Match against two pairs of formidable foes: Cesaro and Sheamus and Luke Gallows and Karl Anderson. After a grueling bout, Kingston hit Sheamus with his dynamic finishing maneuver, Trouble in Paradise, and pinned the Irishman for the win. Case closed.

Unfortunately for The New Day, their victory celebration wouldn't go nearly as well. While the party was poppin' backstage, so were the champagne corks, which led to *Raw* General

Manager Stephanie McMahon getting doused with bubbly. Later that evening, the irate GM would force Big E, Kofi, and Xavier to defend the titles in yet another Triple Threat Tag Team Match. This time, however, their opponents would consist of even more crackerjack competition in the form of Chris Jericho and Kevin Owens as well as Roman Reigns and Seth Rollins.

Despite the seemingly insurmountable odds, ya boys would manage to post yet another "W" when, during the tumultuous match, the bond between their opponents began to fray. Amid the quarreling, The New Day's connection remained steadfast, allowing Xavier to eventually drape his arm over a temporarily immobile Jericho for the three-count.

The New Day then got the party started...again. Before the bubbly could burst, however, the trio reflected on the rocky road they had traveled to ultimately become the longest-reigning tag team in WWE history. "The fact that we got [to this point] is quite remarkable when you consider the origins," Big E said after the match. "It was quite rough." To say the least.

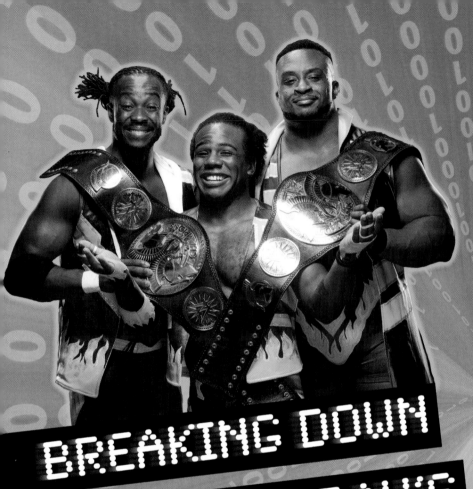

BREAKING DOWN THE NEW DAY'S HISTORIC TITLE REIGN

A lot can happen in 483 days. We analyzed every second of The New Day's landmark Tag Team Title reign, inputted it into a sentient supercomputer and came up with these facts and figures that beautifully illustrate the awe-inspiring nature of ya boys' record-breaking run. The numbers don't lie!

The Longest-Reigning Tag Team Champions In WWE History

258 DAYS

280 DAYS

274 DAYS

279 DAYS

294 DAYS

Mr. Fuji & Mr. Saito

The Colóns

The Hart Foundation

Adrian Adonis & Dick Murdoch

The British Bulldogs

10 **9** **8** **7** **6**

331 DAYS

337 DAYS

370 DAYS

478 DAYS

483 DAYS

Paul London & Brian Kendrick

Mr Fuji & Professor Tanaka

The Valiant Brothers

Demolition

The New Day

5

4

3

2

1

NEW DAY'S REIGN | BY THE NUMBERS

DAYS AS CHAMPIONS	483
HOURS AS CHAMPIONS	
MINUTES AS CHAMPIONS	
SECONDS AS CHAMPIONS	
TELEVISED TAG TEAM MATCHES	44
WINS	25
LOSSES	19
TEAMS FACED	17
LONGEST MATCH	20:20
SHORTEST MATCH	1:20

11,592

695,520

4,1731,200

THE FREEBIRD RULE

God bless The Fabulous Freebirds. The legendary trio of rock 'n' roll outlaws consisting of Michael "P.S." Hayes, Buddy "Jack" Roberts, and Terry "Bam Bam" Gordy innovated "The Freebird Rule" back in the early 1980s whereby all three team members were recognized as tag team champions. Teams like Demolition and The Midnight Express would take advantage of this loophole in later years, but no group did it with as much success as The New Day.

Thanks to the beauty of "The Freebird Rule," all three members of The New Day were recognized as champions, and any two members of the trio were allowed to defend the titles at any time. Here's how the combinations broke down during their record run.

Big E + Kofi Kingston = **33** matches

Xavier Woods + Big E = **6** matches

Kofi Kingston + Xavier Woods = **5** matches

EVERY TELEVISED TAG TEAM MATCH OF THE NEW DAY'S 483-DAY REIGN

BIG E & KOFI KINGSTON DEFEAT CESARO & SHEAMUS AND KARL ANDERSON & LUKE GALLOWS
Raw, December 12, 2016
Wells Fargo Center in
Philadelphia, Pennsylvania, USA

1

BIG E & XAVIER WOODS DEFEATED CHRIS JERICHO & KEVIN OWENS AND ROMAN REIGNS & SETH ROLLINS
Raw, December 12, 2016
Wells Fargo Center in
Philadelphia, Pennsylvania, USA

2

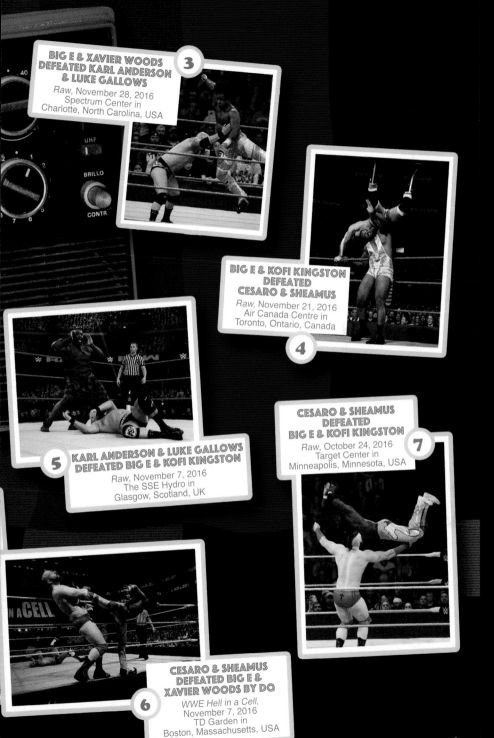

BIG E & XAVIER WOODS DEFEATED KARL ANDERSON & LUKE GALLOWS
Raw, November 28, 2016
Spectrum Center in
Charlotte, North Carolina, USA

3

BIG E & KOFI KINGSTON DEFEATED CESARO & SHEAMUS
Raw, November 21, 2016
Air Canada Centre in
Toronto, Ontario, Canada

4

KARL ANDERSON & LUKE GALLOWS DEFEATED BIG E & KOFI KINGSTON
Raw, November 7, 2016
The SSE Hydro in
Glasgow, Scotland, UK

5

CESARO & SHEAMUS DEFEATED BIG E & KOFI KINGSTON
Raw, October 24, 2016
Target Center in
Minneapolis, Minnesota, USA

7

CESARO & SHEAMUS DEFEATED BIG E & XAVIER WOODS BY DQ
WWE Hell in a Cell,
November 7, 2016
TD Garden in
Boston, Massachusetts, USA

6

BIG E & XAVIER WOODS DEFEATED CHRIS JERICHO & KEVIN OWENS

Raw, October 3, 2016
Staples Center in
Los Angeles, California, USA

8

BIG E & KOFI KINGSTON DEFEATED KARL ANDERSON & LUKE GALLOWS

Raw, September 26, 2016
US Bank Arena in
Cincinnati, Ohio, USA

9

KARL ANDERSON & LUKE GALLOWS DEFEATED KOFI KINGSTON & XAVIER WOODS BY DQ

SummerSlam, August 26, 2016
Barclays Center in
New York City, New York, USA

12

KOFI KINGSTON & XAVIER WOODS DEFEATED THE DUDLEY BOYZ

Raw, August 15, 2016
American Bank Center in
Corpus Christi, Texas, USA

13

BIG E & KOFI KINGSTON DEFEATED BIG CASS & ENZO AMORE, KARL ANDERSON & LUKE GALLOWS AND THE VAUDEVILLAINS

WWE Money in the Bank, June 19, 2016
T-Mobile Arena in
Las Vegas, Nevada, USA

16

10

BIG E & KOFI KINGSTON DEFEATED KARL ANDERSON & LUKE GALLOWS

Clash of the Champions, September 25, 2016 Bankers Life Fieldhouse in Indianapolis, Indiana, USA

11

KARL ANDERSON & LUKE GALLOWS DEFEATED KOFI KINGSTON & XAVIER WOODS

Raw, September 12, 2016 Royal Farms Arena in Baltimore, Maryland, USA

BIG E & KOFI KINGSTON DEFEATED THE VAUDEVILLAINS

SmackDown, June 21, 2016 Tucson Convention Center in Tucson, Arizona, USA

15

14

BIG E & KOFI KINGSTON DEFEATED KARL ANDERSON & LUKE GALLOWS

Raw, August 1, 2016 Philips Arena in Atlanta, Georgia, USA

BIG E & XAVIER WOODS DEFEATED THE VAUDEVILLAINS

WWE Extreme Rules, May 22, 2016, Prudential Center in Newark, New Jersey, USA

17

THE DUDLEY BOYZ DEFEATED BIG E & KOFI KINGSTON

Raw, May 9, 2016 CenturyLink Center Omaha in Omaha, Nebraska, USA

18

19

BIG E & KOFI KINGSTON DEFEATED THE ASCENSION

WWE Main Event, April 5, 2016
Toyota Center in
Houston, Texas, USA

BIG E & KOFI KINGSTON DEFEATED KING BARRETT & SHEAMUS

Raw, April 4, 2016
American Airlines Center in
Dallas, Texas, USA

20

AJ STYLES & CHRIS JERICHO DEFEATED BIG E & KOFI KINGSTON

Raw, February 29, 2016
Bridgestone Arena in
Nashville, Tennessee, USA

24

BIG E & KOFI KINGSTON DEFEATED AJ STYLES & CHRIS JERICHO

Raw, March 7, 2016
Allstate Arena in
Rosemont, Illinois, USA

23

THE USOS DEFEATED BIG E & KOFI KINGSTON

Raw, January 11, 2016
Smoothie King Center in
New Orleans, Louisiana, USA

27

BIG E & KOFI KINGSTON DEFEATED THE LUCHA DRAGONS

SmackDown, December 22, 2015
Wells Fargo Arena in
Des Moines, Iowa, USA

28

21

BIG E & XAVIER WOODS DEFEATED ALBERTO DEL RIO & RUSEV

Raw, March 14, 2016
CONSOL Energy Center in
Pittsburgh, Pennsylvania, USA

22

BIG E & KOFI KINGSTON DEFEATED KING BARRETT & SHEAMUS

WWE Roadblock, March 12, 2016
Ricoh Coliseum in
Toronto, Ontario, Canada

25

DEAN AMBROSE & ROMAN REIGNS DEFEATED BIG E & KOFI KINGSTON

Raw, February 1, 2016
Legacy Arena in
Birmingham, Alabama, USA

26

BIG E & KOFI KINGSTON DEFEATED THE USOS

Royal Rumble, January 24, 2016
Amway Center in
Orlando, Florida, USA

29

THE LUCHA DRAGONS DEFEATED KOFI KINGSTON & XAVIER WOODS

SmackDown, December 15, 2015
Prudential Center in
Newark, New Jersey, USA

30

BIG E & KOFI KINGSTON DEFEATED THE LUCHA DRAGONS AND THE USOS IN A TRIPLE THREAT LADDER MATCH

WWE TLC: Tables, Ladders & Chairs,
December 13, 2015 TD Garden in
Boston, Massachusetts, USA

THE LUCHA DRAGONS DEFEATED KOFI KINGSTON & XAVIER WOODS

SmackDown, December 8, 2015
Jacksonville Veterans Memorial Arena in Jacksonville, Florida, USA

31

32

THE LUCHA DRAGONS DEFEATED BIG E & KOFI KINGSTON

Raw, December 7, 2015
North Charleston Coliseum in North Charleston, South Carolina, USA

BIG E & KOFI KINGSTON DEFEATED DEAN AMBROSE & RANDY ORTON

Raw, October 12, 2015
Allstate Arena in Rosemont, Illinois, USA

36

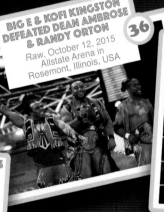

DEAN AMBROSE & ROMAN REIGNS DEFEATED BIG E & KOFI KINGSTON

SmackDown, October 20, 2015
Frank Erwin Center in Austin, Texas, USA

35

BIG E & KOFI KINGSTON DEFEATED THE PRIME TIME PLAYERS

Raw, September 14, 2015
FedExForum in Memphis, Tennessee, USA

39

40

DEAN AMBROSE & ROMAN REIGNS DEFEATED BIG E & KOFI KINGSTON BY DQ

SmackDown, September 1, 2015
American Airlines Arena in Miami, Florida, USA

**BIG E & KOFI KINGSTON
DEFEATED
THE DUDLEY BOYZ**

WWE Hell in a Cell, October 25, 2015
Staples Center in
Los Angeles, California, USA

34

**THE LUCHA DRAGONS
DEFEATED BIG E
& KOFI KINGSTON**

SmackDown, November 24, 2015
Bankers Life Fieldhouse in
Indianapolis, Indiana, USA

33

**THE DUDLEY BOYZ
DEFEATED BIG E &
KOFI KINGSTON BY DQ**

WWE Live from MSG, October 3, 2015
Madison Square Garden in
New York City, New York, USA

37

**THE DUDLEY BOYZ
DEFEATED
BIG E & KOFI KINGSTON BY DQ**

Night of Champions, September 20, 2015
Toyota Center in
Houston, Texas, USA

38

**THE DUDLEY BOYZ
DEFEATED BIG E & KOFI KINGSTON**

Raw, August 31, 2015,
Amalie Arena in Tampa, Florida, USA

41

42

BIG E & KOFI KINGSTON
MATADORES,

NEW DAY'S RIVALS

The New Day took on all comers during their historic championship run. Here are all the teams who tried to knock the kings off their throne, including one lucky team who succeeded.

| Karl Anderson & Luke Gallows | **9** MATCHES | The Lucha Dragons | **7** MATCHES | The Dudley Boyz | **6** MATCHES |

| Cesaro & Sheamus | **4** MATCHES | The Vaudevillains | **4** MATCHES | The Usos | **3** MATCHES |

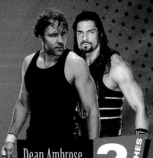

Dean Ambrose & Roman Reigns **3** MATCHES

AJ Styles & Chris Jericho **2** MATCHES

King Barrett & Sheamus **2** MATCHES

The Prime Time Players **2** MATCHES

Chris Jericho & Kevin Owens **2** MATCHES

Big Cass & Enzo Amore **1** MATCHE

Roman Reigns & Seth Rollins **1** MATCHE

The Ascension **1** MATCHE

Alberto Del Rio & Rusev **1** MATCHE

Dean Ambrose & Randy Orton **1** MATCHE

Los Matadores **1** MATCHE

THE MOST MAGICAL CHAMPIONSHIP EVER MADE

You know you've made it when you get your own custom title. Only 483 of these exquisite, unicorn-adorned Tag Team Title replicas were created to recognize The New Day's 483-day reign.

They even sold for $483 a pop on WWEShop. A pittance for a piece of history.

PRE-POSITIVITY

It seems unfathomable to imagine The New Day as anything other than a cohesive three-man unit. But long before embarking on their quest to purge WWE of negativity, each member was a successful Superstar in his own right. Before diving headlong into their Technicolor journey, let's recognize the early years of three multi-talented individuals forging their path through sports entertainment...

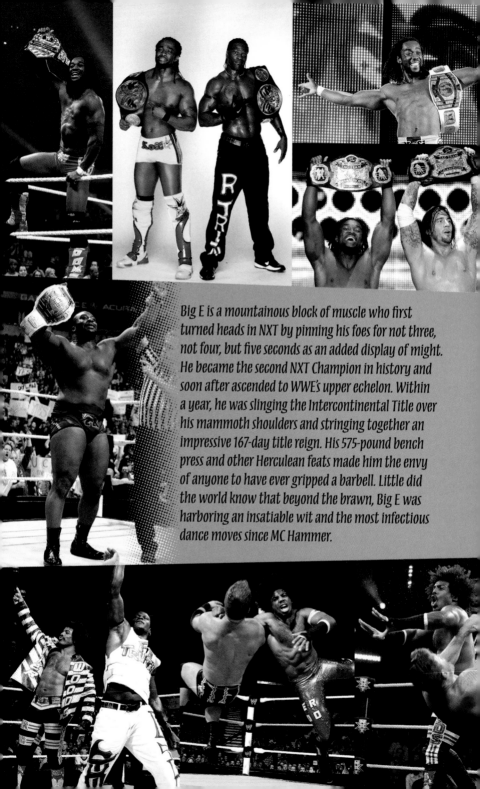

Big E is a mountainous block of muscle who first turned heads in NXT by pinning his foes for not three, not four, but five seconds as an added display of might. He became the second NXT Champion in history and soon after ascended to WWE's upper echelon. Within a year, he was slinging the Intercontinental Title over his mammoth shoulders and stringing together an impressive 167-day title reign. His 575-pound bench press and other Herculean feats made him the envy of anyone to have ever gripped a barbell. Little did the world know that beyond the brawn, Big E was harboring an insatiable wit and the most infectious dance moves since MC Hammer.

Even before his New Day success, Kofi Kingston was one of the most decorated Superstars in WWE. Kofi brought his boundless energy and mind-boggling athleticism to the big stage in 2008. Six years and countless gravity-defying highlights later, Kofi had racked up five Intercontinental Championships, three United States Championships, and Tag Team Title reigns alongside CM Punk, Evan Bourne, and R-Truth. Along the way, he became notorious for escape tactics in the Royal Rumble Match that would have left the great Houdini bewildered. Despite joining The New Day as its most senior Superstar, Kofi wholly embraced the group's roundtable mentality.

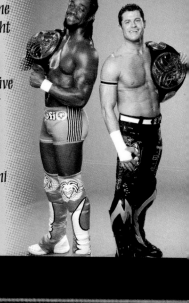

Xavier Woods was a high-octane competitor for several years before joining WWE. Beginning in NXT, he outfitted himself with retro-90s flair between the yellow ropes. The classic gaming aficionado displayed agility fit for the cast of Mortal Kombat, and with academic credits toward a Ph.D, can school opponents with his mind as well. Looking to find his footing on WWE's main roster, Woods briefly sided with R-Truth. However, it soon became clear that to reach the heights that he craved, his career needed a new direction. Woods decided it was time to unleash his true personality on the WWE Universe. But first he needed to find the right partners to share in his vision...

DAWNING OF

The Wright brothers took four years to achieve flight. It was thirty-two years after Mount Everest was mapped that Sir Edmund Hillary and Tenzing Norgay conquered the world's highest peak. And Chinese dynasties labored for more than 2,000 years to build that country's Great Wall. Many of history's monumental achievements have taken time, effort, and more than a little perseverance. The New Day's rise to the top is no exception.

In the summer of 2014, Big E and Kofi teamed up as tag partners with decidedly mixed results. After suffering a string of disheartening defeats, the pair was confronted by Xavier, who told them in no uncertain terms that they would never achieve championship status by "kissing babies and shaking hands." The following night, X-Man would cheer a reenergized Big E and Kofi to victory from ringside during WWE's *Main Event*. That fateful evening, the group gave the world a glimpse of the greatness

THE NEW DAY

After a three-month hiatus from television, the trio reemerged in November, appearing in promotional videos on *Monday Night Raw* under the moniker The New Day. The videos featured the men dressed in suits standing before a gospel choir that sang their praises.

And though, inside the ring, The New Day was picking up decisive wins, outside the squared circle they were quickly racking up scalding criticism. Their new look and feel grated on fans almost immediately. The group's attempts to lead the audience in chants of "New Day rocks!" were quickly hijacked and turned into chants of "New Day sucks!" It was a mantra that garnered a foothold among the WWE Universe and began to resonate throughout arenas wherever New Day appeared.

Adding to the trio's frustration, their philosophy—banking heavily on "the power of positivity"—was unceremoniously mocked by fans and some WWE commentators alike. If drastic steps weren't taken, the sun was about to abruptly set on The New Day

QUIZ TIME: HOW WELL DO YOU KNOW THE NEW DAY?

BRAIN POWER IS IMPORTANT, BUT BEFORE JUMPING TO THE THEORETICAL PHYSICS SECTION OF THE BOOK, LET'S TEST YOUR KNOWLEDGE OF THE NEW DAY WITH THE "KNEW DAY QUIZ." SEE WHAT WE DID THERE?

1. The New Day beat Cesaro and Tyson Kidd to become WWE Tag Team Champions in 2015 at what event?
   - A. *Extreme Rules*
   - B. *SummerSlam*
   - C. *Fastlane*
   - D. *Payback*

2. Although all three of The New Day were integral in the victory, which two members were the official participants in this match?
   - A. Kofi Kingston and Xavier Woods
   - B. Big E and Kofi Kingston
   - C. Xavier Woods and Big E

3. The New Day's reign as champions came to an end at *WWE Money in the Bank* in what many believe to be the darkest day in sports-entertainment history. Who beat them?

    A. The Prime Time Players
    B. The Usos
    C. The Dudley Boyz
    D. The Lucha Dragons

4. Kofi was a three-time Tag Team Champion before joining The New Day. Which partner did he NOT win the championships with?

    A. Evan Bourne
    B. CM Punk
    C. John Morrison
    D. R-Truth

5. On the November 2, 2015, edition of *Raw*, The New Day teamed up with Seth Rollins and which other Superstar for a Traditional Survivor Series Match?

    A. Triple H
    B. Kevin Owens
    C. Kane
    D. Big Show

6. Which New Day member had a 166-day reign as Intercontinental Champion?

    A. Big E

    B. Kofi Kingston

    C. Xavier Woods

    D. Francesca II: Turbo

7. Which celebrity served as The New Day's guest manager at *SummerSlam 2016* despite a track record on this stage that was spotty at best?

    A. Wale

    B. Jon Stewart

    C. Grumpy Cat

    D. Dr. Phil

8. Which hashtag did The New Day popularize during their 2015 molly-whopping of The Dudley Boyz?

    A. #DownWithECW

    B. #SaveTheTables

    C. #BoyzArentMen

    D. #SayNoToCamouflage

9. Which three members of The League of Booty did The New Day battle at *WrestleMania 32*?

    A. Alberto Del Rio, Bad News Barrett, and Rusev

    B. Bad News Barrett, Sheamus, and Rusev

    C. Rusev, Sheamus, and Alberto Del Rio

    D. Sheamus, Alberto Del Rio, and Bad News Barrett

10. How many *WrestleMania* victories have The New Day achieved as a unit?

    A. Three

    B. Two

    C. One

    D. Zero

Answers: 1.A, 2.B, 3.A, 4.C, 5.B, 6.A, 7.B, 8.B, 9.C, 10.D

XAVIER WOODS' GUIDE TO FOLLICLE FABULOUSNESS

Nobody has a better mane than Xavier Woods. It's lush, it's full, and he can do anything with it. Here, Xavier shares the inspirations behind three of his most spectacular hair days.

The Michelle Obama

If you appreciate a strong woman (and if you don't then that's a discussion for a different time) then you should appreciate the fact that one of the hardest things for them to drop into their schedules is a hair appointment. This 'do pays homage to all the powerful females out there who only have time to hit their hair with the hot comb. No curls, no pizazz, just business—and they look good doing it. This is a very powerful coif considering the fact that it was rocked by a First Lady and also Katt Williams. Both extremely successful people in their own regard. (Let's just ignore the fact that Katt Williams got knocked out by a child.)

The Rufio

For this hairstyle to work you must realize a few different things. First, you have to understand the history of the false legend Peter Pan. People revere him as a hero but in reality he's the villain. He steals the souls of children and keeps them locked away on his island. Hook is the only child that ever escaped and has been on a quest to end Peter Pan so no other children will suffer. Rufio's soul was taken by Peter Pan later than souls usually are taken. This made it easier for him to see who Pan really was. So when Peter Pan left the island, Rufio took over to try and help the lost souls. Upon Peter Pan's return Rufio was going to confront him but Peter Pan got in his head and sent him to fight Hook. This is why Hook had no choice but to end the life of Rufio. A sad, sad tale, but understanding it is the only way to honestly pay homage to the boy known as Rufio, Rufio, Ru-Fi-OOOOOO.

The Gaston

Similar to the misconception of Peter Pan, Gaston from *Beauty and the Beast* is revered as a villain when he really was the hero. A man who was the greatest hunter of his time (had to work to get there). Jacked, meaning he worked out and took care of his body. Good looking, every woman in the town wanted him and all the men wanted to be him. He wanted Belle, a human who was essentially garbage considering the fact that she brought nothing of worth to her community. She sat around all day doing nothing. Yes, she read, which is good, but she never once applied the knowledge that she was supposedly getting from these stories she was reading. Gaston—who was a stand-up guy—turned down the triplets (TRIPLETS!) because he only wanted to be with this complete bore. What a gentleman. He then saw she was in danger and had been kidnapped by a beast, so he went to save her and defeat the hideous monster so that it wouldn't abduct anyone else in the town that he loved. But people say he is the villain? Incorrect. People should understand that he is the greatest Disney hero ever, which is why I decided to pay homage to him with this immaculate coiffure.

THE NEW DAY
FORGE A DIFFERENT PATH FORWARD

In the wake of their chilly reception, New Day was faced with a choice: Either continue on a path that seemed destined for failure or reinvent themselves yet again. With nothing to lose, the group promptly set out to recalculate their route. Rather than the path preordained for them, the trio instead chose the road not yet traveled.

Steadily, they began to incorporate their own personalities into promos, sprinkling in hobbies that interested them and topics that made them laugh as they spent time traveling together.

In 2015, Xavier began bringing a trombone he had named Francesca to the ring during the group's entrance. He would even play it during matches in an effort to rouse the crowd into a "New Day rocks!" chant—and an unusual thing happened. The unorthodox efforts started to pay dividends. Crowds were slowly won over and began to get behind the newly untethered trio.

Later that year, The New Day incorporated a unicorn into their aesthetic, even adorning merchandise with the mystical creature. This would soon lead to the group wearing actual plastic unicorn horns to the ring during their entrance. When these horns became available to the WWE Universe, crowds would be brimming with the plastic protrusions.

By the time the trio introduced the word "booty," the influence of The New Day had become undeniable. The word quickly found its way into the sports-entertainment lexicon as a means to describe something or someone less than desirable. Big E, Kofi, and Xavier often employed it to great effect to scorch opponents.

This fresh, irreverent incarnation of The New Day had steadily converted fans and critics alike. Now, Big E, Kofi, and Xavier, who had once suffered blistering reviews, were finally earning the respect and accolades they worked so hard to achieve.

What are your favorite sports teams?

Anything and everything Boston—Red Sox, Celtics, Bruins, even the New England Revolution and I don't even know anything about soccer. And speaking of "futbol," there's the mighty New England Patriots. The greatest team in the history of sports. Fun fact: in Super Bowl XLI, the New England Patriots staged the greatest comeback in the history of sports when they rallied back from a 28–3 deficit to win the game 34–28. They beat the Atlanta Falcons...Xavier's team. Xavier's reaction during the game can be seen here:

Do you have any pets?

I have a Shih Tzu Maltese and a Chihuahua Dachshund. They have a combined weight of 12.5 lbs. Don't judge me... like everyone else does when they see me walking them. I've literally had people stop their cars to laugh at me as I walk my little dogs.

Did you have any nicknames growing up?

People called me "Supafly"...no they didn't. But I wanted them to. I even changed my AIM screen name to SupaflyKSM in hopes that it would catch on. It didn't. Kofi is such a unique name so the best I ever got was Kof.

What was your favorite school subject?

English. I love words and literature.

Whom did you idolize growing up?

I don't think I idolized anyone in particular growing up. I was enamored and obsessed with WWE from elementary school through college. I joined the high school wrestling team thinking that it was WWE wrestling.

Do you have any weird pet peeves?

When you get to a public urinal and there's puddles of pee on the floor. It's like, I mean...you made it to your destination. You made it. Literally standing over your target, and you just... pee on the floor?! Just awful.

What is your favorite food?

My wife's pancakes

Least favorite?

Anything to do with pork or beef

Can you share a story of a crazy interaction with a fan?

We always get pictures on social media from people who have tattooed our logo or even our faces on their skin. This is crazy to me, knowing that we have such a profound effect on people that they are willing to wear our likeness on themselves forever! Blessed to be in a position to have such a positive effect on people's lives. The Power of Positivity is real!

GET TO KNOW THE NEW DAY UNIVERSE

The New Day may be the most dynamic trio in the history of WWE, but there's more to this holy trinity than just Kofi, Big E, and Woods. A host of characters both magical and musical inhabit the New Day Universe and help the boys spread wonder across the globe.

POWER OF POSITIVITY

THE NEW DAY

THE MUSIC

FRANCESCA

The group's official fourth member, this trombone helped create the initial New Day phenomena as Woods' bleats before, during, and after matches quickly became a fan favorite element of any New Day appearance. It's easy to forget, but some fans were still booing the team when Francesca first debuted at SummerSlam in Brooklyn, N.Y., where the trio performed a loving, if not slightly offensive, rendition of "New York, New York." Unfortunately, Francesca was destroyed by Chris Jericho in a gruesome act that he has yet to be prosecuted for.

Francesca

FRANCESCA FACT:

During Francesca's tearful funeral on *Raw*, Woods vowed to avenge his fallen trombone by "eating hella Chipotle," then defiling the bathroom of Chris Jericho. It's unclear whether or not this actually ended up happening, but Jericho should be wary of inviting Woods to his next dinner party.

FRANCESCA II: TURBO

Although Woods was heartbroken following the demise of Francesca, he would not be silenced. At the 2016 Royal Rumble, where The New Day defeated The Usos, Xavier revealed his new trombone, Francesca II: Turbo. Oiled up and blessed with a sweet Street Fighter-inspired name, this trombone made Woods' heart sing, even if she did cheat on him with Enzo Amore. Sadly, Francesca II: Turbo faced a similar fate to her predecessor, and was eventually destroyed by the ginger hands of Sheamus.

AGNES

When *Raw* emanated from the SSE Hydro in Glasgow, Scotland, on November 7, 2016, The New Day introduced another member of their musical family—a pair of bagpipes named Agnes. Francesca's Scottish cousin helped The New Day antagonize Sheamus with a hilarious spoof of the movie *Braveheart*, although Woods never quite got a handle on how to play them.

BIG E'S TOP 10 MUSICAL ARTISTES

Big K.R.I.T. 10

A$AP Ferg 9

Florence & The Machine 8

Cannibal Ox 7

Ghostface Killah 6

Nas 5

Wale 4

Flatbush Zombies 3

Blu 2

1 Tupac

The Magic

G. MOORE BUTTZ THE UNICORN

Magical. Mythical. Majestic. The unicorn exists on a higher level of consciousness, transcending the worries and trivialities of mere mortals. Some people may tell you the unicorn never existed, but The New Day know better and have chosen it as their spirit animal. Why? Well, for a long time, there wasn't much magic in the world of WWE. That all changed when The New Day came along. You might even say they're the unicorns of WWE. And they've got the horns to prove it.

UNICORNS: THE LOWDOWN

In 2012, North Korea's government "news" agency reported that scientists had "reconfirmed" the existence and location of the final resting place of the unicorn ridden by ancient King Tongmyong nearly six hundred years earlier. There's no good reason to trust madcap dictator Kim Jong-un, but in this case he's gotta be right!

WHOOLIO THE OWL

With wisdom as its defining characteristic, the owl knows when to speak and when to keep its counsel. As a result of superior intellect, the owl is convinced it's pretty much better than everyone else. The nerve, right? But before you condemn this animal for arrogance, realize that—let's be honest—it probably is way smarter than you.

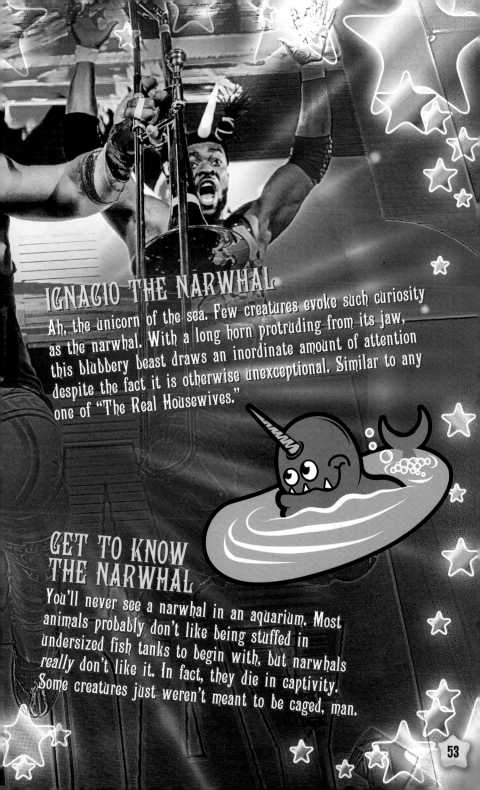

IGNACIO THE NARWHAL

Ah, the unicorn of the sea. Few creatures evoke such curiosity as the narwhal. With a long horn protruding from its jaw, this blubbery beast draws an inordinate amount of attention despite the fact it is otherwise unexceptional. Similar to any one of "The Real Housewives."

GET TO KNOW THE NARWHAL

You'll never see a narwhal in an aquarium. Most animals probably don't like being stuffed in undersized fish tanks to begin with, but narwhals really don't like it. In fact, they die in captivity. Some creatures just weren't meant to be caged, man.

FINDING YOUR SPIRIT ANIMAL

RAINBOW CATCHERS

The Power of Positivity

Cotton Candy

Happy Thoughts

THE NAPES OF WRATH

A TAIL OF TWO BOOTIES

THE CANDY CORN

THE SWEET TOOTH

Dessert Sweets Pies Cakes

Piggyback Rides

Booty O'S

Clapping

New Day Rocks

Cats Wearing Mittens

Laughter

Magic

Sprinkles

The Bees Knees

Being Tickled Pink

A CHILD'S WONDER

DANCING SHOES

You've just met the three sacred spirit animals in the New Day universe: The narwhal, the owl, and the unicorn. To determine which most accurately represents you, indicate the number, on a scale of 1–5, that most truthfully reflects how you feel about the following statements.

1 You have crazy, wild mood swings. But only because it's fun to keep people guessing.

STRONGLY AGREE   ① ② ③ ④ ⑤   STRONGLY DISAGREE

2 You'd rather not follow through with a plan if it wasn't yours to begin with. Besides, your ideas are always better . . . Always.

STRONGLY AGREE ①②③④⑤ STRONGLY DISAGREE

3 You like to draw attention to yourself—'cause you're super interesting and entertaining that way.

STRONGLY AGREE ①②③④⑤ STRONGLY DISAGREE

4 You're quick to take revenge on anyone who wrongs you, especially the idiotic ones.

STRONGLY AGREE ①②③④⑤ STRONGLY DISAGREE

5 You enjoy complimenting others—only because you know they'll feel obliged to compliment you in return.

STRONGLY AGREE ①②③④⑤ STRONGLY DISAGREE

6 You can be absent-minded. While at other times you can be . . . Wait. What was the question again?

STRONGLY AGREE ①②③④⑤ STRONGLY DISAGREE

7 You misdirect strangers who ask for directions because they should know better—and it's hilarious watching them circle the block.

STRONGLY AGREE ①②③④⑤ STRONGLY DISAGREE

8 You always have to check a mirror before leaving the house to make certain you're on fleek. And you always are. Naturally.

STRONGLY AGREE ①②③④⑤ STRONGLY DISAGREE

To see which spirit animal will accompany you on your life path, add the numbers you selected from the quiz. Take that total and match it to your spirit animal below.

0-13	14-27	28-40
The Narwhal	The Owl	The Unicorn

BOOTY-O'S:
THEY MAKE SURE YOU AIN'T BOOTY

HOW MANY OTHER SUPERSTARS DO YOU KNOW WITH THEIR OWN BREAKFAST CEREAL? THERE'S NO HONEY BUNCHES OF USO ON YOUR SUPERMARKET SHELF. NOT EVEN ANY CENA FLAKES. BUT THERE ARE BOOTY-O'S.

BOOTY-O'S MARSHMALLOW TREATS

WWE Digital correspondent Cathy Kelley cooked up this recipe for Booty-O's Marshmallow Treats. These make Rice Krispy Treats look like a pile of dog food. The lousy kind of dog food they give to bad dogs. Not that good stuff full of nutrients they give to fancy show dogs.

Ingredients: One box of Booty-O's, ½ cup of butter, 10 oz. of mini marshmallows

Step 1: Melt ½ cup butter over low-to-medium heat.

Step 2: Add 10 oz. of mini marshmallows. Stir until smooth.

Step 3: Turn heat to low, add a box of Booty-O's, stir until all that deliciousness is mixed together.

Step 4: Pour that into a 9x13 casserole dish, spread evenly, let sit for 30 minutes to an hour.

Step 5: Watch *Animaniacs* on Netflix while your treats cool.

Step 6: Eat that goodness!

RAINBOW FACT

The world's longest-observed rainbow was spotted over Sheffield, England, on March 14, 1994, where it radiated from roughly 9 a.m. to 3 p.m. That's six hours of pure, unadulterated positivity!

THE NEW DAY

THE NEW DAY HIT THEIR STRIDE

By early 2015, just six months after X-Man teamed with Big E and Kofi, The New Day had earned impressive wins against such squads as The Ascension, Gold and Stardust, and The Wyatt Family. Their biggest victory to date, however, was yet to come.

After nearly a year of proving themselves, The New Day finally earned a WWE Tag Team Championship Match at the *Extreme Rules* pay-per-view on April 26, 2015. They would be facing Cesaro and Tyson Kidd, the reigning champions and a fiercely formidable duo.

The crowd inside Chicago's Allstate Arena was itching for the bout that would see Big E and Kofi compete for New Day as Xavier backed them from ringside. In an early indication of just how difficult New Day's task would be, the unbelievably strong Cesaro caught the 285-pound Big E in mid-air and slammed The New Day wrecking ball to the mat. Later, Kofi would attempt Trouble in Paradise on Kidd only to have the ring technician reverse the move into a Sharpshooter.

In the end, however, New Day would prevail with a little assistance from Xavier. The New Day's hype-man distracted Kidd, allowing Big E to toss the athletic Superstar off the ring apron. Kofi, the legal man, then seized Cesaro and pinned him for the win, kicking off The New Day's first WWE Tag Team Championship reign.

QUIZ TIME: TRUE OR FALSE?

THE NEW DAY DID NOT ATTAIN A SUPREME LEVEL OF POSITIVITY BY SPOUTING FALSEHOODS. NEITHER SHOULD YOU! SCAN THROUGH THE BELOW AND WEED OUT ALL FIBS, FABRICATIONS, AND GENERAL NONSENSE.

1. Big E debuted in WWE by attacking Randy Orton.

2. The New Day won the first ever Tag Team Elimination Chamber Match.

3. The New Day was originally managed by WWE Hall of Famer Paul Ellering.

4. The New Day won their second Tag Team Championship in a Triple Threat Match at *SummerSlam 2015.*

5. In their first-ever Ladder Match competing as a team, The New Day defeated the Lucha Dragons and The Usos to defend the WWE Tag Team Championships.

6. Wielding their authority as hosts of *WrestleMania 33*, The New Day shocked the WWE Universe by inserting the legendary team of Edge and Christian into the Ladder Match for the Raw Tag Team Championship.

7. After defeating the Usos in July of 2017, The New Day became the first team to have held both the Raw and *SmackDown* Tag Team Championships.

8. Big E's first tag team partner in WWE was Dolph Ziggler.

9. All three members of The New Day competed in NXT prior to joining the main WWE roster.

10. Hip-hop star Wale once hosted a battle rap on *SmackDown* Live where The New Day traded verbal jabs with The Usos.

11. New Day's victory for the *SmackDown* Tag Team Championships in July 2017 was especially sweet for Xavier Woods. The win marked the first time Woods applied the deciding pin for a championship in his career.

12. During *SummerSlam* weekend in 2015, The New Day crooned a parody version of "New York State of Mind" by Billy Joel.

13. At *WrestleMania 32*, The New Day lost their WWE Tag Team Championships to the League of Nations.

14. Xavier Woods once got under Chris Jericho's skin so much that Jericho placed X-Man's name on the famous "List of Jericho" twice.

15. The New Day was the final team to hold the WWE Tag Team Championships before the creation of separate *Raw* and *SmackDown* Championships.

Answers: 1. False (He attacked John Cena.), 2. True, 3. False, 4. False (It was a Fatal Four Way.), 5. True, 6. False (They inserted The Hardy Boyz into the match.), 7. True, 8. True, 9. False (Kofi never competed in NXT), 10. True, 11. True, 12. False (They lampooned "Empire State of Mind" by Jay-Z and "New York, New York." by Frank Sinatra), 13. False (They were defeated, but the titles were not at stake.), 14. True, 15. True

NEW DAY THAT'S WHO!

Who is your favorite e-sports athlete?

Ll Joe—he inspired me to get better at fighting games so I could eventually get better at Tekken.

Do you have any pets?

No, but I'm definitely a cat person. Dogs terrorized me throughout my youth. Growling at me, biting me, chasing me, so I am not too fond of them. But cats. Man, I love cats!

Did you have any nicknames growing up?

My dad used to call me (and still does from time to time) Big A. Which is funny now since I'm friends with Big E. And I used to want my wrestling name to be Zero because many of my favorite things had Zero in the name. Zero was an amazing character in the Megaman series, Zero was the name of Jack Skellington's dog in *The Nightmare Before Christmas*, and in the movie *Hackers* the main character's screen name was Zero Cool, so I just loved Zero.

What was your favorite school subject?

Psychology. I have a Bachelor's degree in Philosophy and Psychology and a Masters in Psychology. I am still striving to get my Ph.D. in psychology at some point. I'd love to work with children dealing with autism to help them with different therapies.

Whom did you idolize growing up?

Growing up Jackie Chan was my idol. His life story is incredible to me and I always wanted to be in some form of entertainment where I could fight but also be comedic. He was the epitome of that. During my teenage years I added Lenny Kravitz to that list and ended up growing my hair out so I could look more like him!

Do you have any weird pet peeves?

There are not enough pages in this book to list them all, but the biggest would probably be when people repeat your answer as a question or question the answer that you give them. For instance, if I say, "I went to the store" and then someone replies, "You went to the store?" then I can't handle it. Another example would be "I went to the store" and someone replies, "Really?" NO, I WAS JUST TELLING YOU I WENT TO THE STORE BECAUSE I FELT LIKE SAYING IT FOR NO REASON WHEN IT WASNT TRUE! YES, I WENT TO THE STORE! DID I STUTTER?!

Is there anything you refuse to eat?

THAT WOULD...sorry, still fired up from the previous question. That would have to be oysters. They feel like you're swallowing a chunk of snot. Disgusting.

Can you share a story about a crazy fan interaction?

We were in Germany once coming down the ramp and I spotted a teenage boy literally crying because he was so excited. Not like a little bit. This boy was full out bawling. I didn't know what to do so I hugged him and he said thank you and we both went about our day.

INSIDE THE WILD WORLD OF UPUPDOWNDOWN

How many people do you know who have their own YouTube channel? Okay, maybe a lot. But how many people do you know who have their own YouTube channel with more than a million subscribers, hundreds of hours of awesome video game content, and a video where Kalisto is fed a spoonful of hot sauce and almost pukes?

Well, Xavier Woods does. As the majordomo of UpUpDownDown, Woods, who goes by the nom de plume Austin Creed on the channel, invites his fellow Superstars, as well as a cavalcade of celebrity guests and popular YouTubers, to mash buttons on video games both old and new.

If you're not yet a loyal subscriber to UUDD, carve out a free weekend and dig into the endless amount of hilarious videos where Superstar personalities shine through, but before you head over to YouTube, read our primer on the most fun place on the internet. Game on!

KNOW YOUR UPUPDOWNDOWN CODENAMES

If you've come to play games on UpUpDownDown, you can check your birth name at the door. Like any secret society worth its salt, everyone who grabs a controller on UUDD gets a codename. That includes Stephanie McMahon, who was dubbed The Queen when she stopped by to play *Streets of Rage*. (Yes, that really happened.)

Check this list of Superstars and their WWE nicknames and see if you can match them up.

1. Kofi Kingston		**A.** The Champ
2. Big E		**B.** The C. Merchandise
3. Seth Rollins		**C.** Mr. UFC
4. Jey Uso		**D.** Tong Po
5. Rusev		**E.** Kicks
6. Curtis Axel		**F.** Pogo
7. Bayley		**G.** Big Wool
8. Naomi		**H.** Battery Man
9. Roman Reigns		**I.** Mr. 24/7
10. Sami Zayn		**J.** Cold Beer

XAVIER'S TOP 10 VIDEO GAME HALL OF FAME

Xavier Woods may have held a championship for 483 consecutive days, but he's probably had a controller in his hand for longer. The man knows games, plain and simple, and these are his ten all-time favorites.

10. Mischief Makers

9. Mega Man 5

8. Mafia III

7. Big Buck Hunter

6. Dance Dance
   Revolution

5. River City Ransom

4. WrestleMania 2000

3. NBA Jam

2. Nights Into Dreams

1. Mario Kart: Double Dash

5 MOST-WATCHED VIDEOS IN UPUPDOWNDOWN HISTORY

5. *Ping Pong Battle!* Cesaro vs. Rusev!—Gamer Gauntlet

1,471,772 views

Highlight:
Rusev announces, "I'm not celebrating, I expected it," after beating Cesaro 21–14.

Believe it or not, the fifth most-watched video in UpUpDownDown history doesn't even feature a video game. Instead, it's an old-school game of ping pong between UUDD favorite Rusev and Cesaro, who hosts his own series on the channel dedicated to the game "Clash of Clans."

4. FIFA 17 Tournament Rd. 1: Roman Reigns vs. Rusev—Gamer Gauntlet

1,800,601 views

Highlight:
Another memorable quote from Rusev, who this time declares, "I'm changing my gamer name to Roman Reigns, because nobody can beat me."

Rusev strikes again. This time, Tong Po takes on Roman Reigns—who goes by the name The Merchandise when guesting on UUDD—in the first round of the *FIFA 2017 Tournament*. After dominating Reigns 3–0, Rusev went on to beat Neville in the finals to win the whole shebang.

3. Bayley vs. Sasha Banks III (*Mortal Kombat X* Makeup Punishment)—Gamer Gauntlet

2,244,797 views

Highlight: The Boss and Bayley kick off the episode with spot-on recreations of some classic Superstar entrances—MVP for Banks and Steve Blackman for Bayley.

Punishments are one of the most entertaining elements of UUDD, and this time it's Pogo—known to WWE fans as Bayley—who suffers the public humiliation of a hideous makeover at the hands of Sasha Banks after falling to her in *Mortal Kombat X*.

2. *Madden 16* Tournament FINALS—Seth Rollins vs. Jack Swagger—Gamer Gauntlet

2,288,100 views

Highlight: It's hard to top the beautiful blue sharkskin suit X wore for this very special occasion.

The only thing more coveted than the WWE Championship in the WWE locker room may be the UUDD Madden Tournament Trophy, which was first claimed by Seth Rollins in this highly entertaining showdown. Rollins, who is fittingly dubbed The Champ on UUDD, also won the second annual tournament. Is there anything that guy can't do?

1. *Call of Duty: Infinite Warfare*: Reigns and Rollins team up with Creed and Kofi!—Superstar Savepoint

2,314,220 views

Highlight: The Slo-Mo Celebration Cam.

You just knew a teamup between The New Day and The Shield was going to be epic. In the most watched UUDD episode ever, Creed, Kofi, Seth, and Roman join forces on the battlefield to wipe out the competition in *Call of Duty: Infinite Warfare*.

UPUPDOWNDOWN PUNISHMENTS

It's not all fun and games on UpUpDownDown. Oftentimes, the stakes are high, and if you lose a game, you pay the price by way of punishments. Here are eight of the most brutal punishments that have been carried out in some of UUDD's most unforgiving moments.

The game: NBA 2K17
The punishment: Put the winner's sock in your mouth
Who got punished? Rich Swann
The punisher: The Brian Kendrick

The game: Mass Effect: Andromeda
The punishment: Drink a Krogan Shake (coffee grounds, popcorn, Goldfish crackers, oats, water, chicken, and rainbow sorbet mixed together in a blender)
Who got punished? Kofi Kingston
The punisher: Ember Moon

The game: Injustice 2
The punishment: Eat a habanero pepper covered in sriracha sauce, and then say nice things about the winner
Who got punished? Sasha Banks
The punisher: Bayley

The game: WWE 2K15
The punishment: Get chopped in the chest while doing pullups
Who got punished? Heath Slater
The punisher: Jimmy Uso

The game: Mortal Kombat X
The punishment: Attempt to swallow a spoonful of cinnamon
Who got punished? Mikaze
The punisher: Xavier Woods

The game: Madden 17
The punishment: Put your hand in a mouse trap
Who got punished? Kofi Kingston
The punisher: Mikaze

The game: Soulcalibur
The punishment: Eat a hot dog covered in mayonnaise
Who got punished? Xavier Woods
The punisher: Giant Bomb's Dan Ryckert

The game: Mortal Kombat X
The punishment: Winner gives the loser a makeover
Who got punished? Bayley
The punisher: Sasha Banks

Get Creative on the Coloring Book Pages

A key to The New Day's success was unabashed self-expression. Show how creative you can be by breaking out a box of crayons and adding some color to The New Day's world—and don't be afraid to color outside the lines.

Dressing To Impress

Might sound trite, but clothes make the man. And kids in some third world country make the clothes. But don't let the ugly realities of international commerce stand in the way of looking good. If you're going to feel positive on the inside, you've got to look halfway decent on the outside. That doesn't mean you've got to be the most stylish guy in town, you've just got to have a style. And as long as you have confidence, you can pull off pretty much anything. Unless you're naked wearing black dress socks. That never looks good, bruh.

As three men who've spent a great deal of their adult lives in spandex, New Day nonetheless managed to sell so much clothing you'd think they worked at TJ Maxx. Currently, here's what's taking up space in their shared closet in The New Day manor:

Spandex. Lots of spandex.

Honestly, we're not sure how spandex isn't currently hugging the curves of every man, woman, and child on this planet. Ever notice how everybody's wearing spandex jumpsuits in sci-fi movies about the future? Why do you think that is? There's no running from tomorrow, so embrace it before everyone else does.

142 New Day T-shirts

Most T-shirts in the New Day closet have pictures of Big E, Kofi, and Xavier on them, which is pretty strange when you stop and think about it. You can wear a shirt with a picture of ya boys on it (they get a cut of the merchandise sales, so that'd be sweet), or you can go down to the local print shop and have them create a couple of tees with your mug on the front. People on the street might even think you're somebody famous.

12 matching tracksuits

If New Day could spend every minute of their lives in tracksuits, they might. The great thing about tracksuits is they make you look like an incredibly active individual even if you just threw one on to make a Chipotle run. You may have a burrito bowl and a large Sprite in your hands, but people still might mistake you for an Italian soccer star.

3 matching suits

New Day rarely get to wear these suits, which is unfortunate, because they look great in them. That's mostly why they wanted us to include this entry so they'd show that dope pic of them all murdered out in evening wear. Plus, their moms like to see them dressed up.

3 kilts

How are these not more popular?
New Day brought three back from
their trip to Glasgow and can
hardly believe the comfort, the
mobility, the jolt of energy you
get while wearing one! Those
big burly Scotsmen really have
it all figured out. They look like
total beasts you'd never want
to mess with, so no one says
anything about the fact that
they're wearing skirts with
no underwear. They're truly
living the dream. Forget
spandex, kilts should be the
style of the future.

98 pairs of
New Day socks

Remember back when everyone (and
that may include you) was chanting "New
Day sucks!"? Fast-forward a few months,
and all of a sudden those same haters
are wearing New Day socks. It was New
Day's idea for it, but damn, it must be
weird knowing your face is all dug up in
somebody's corns and bunions. Yeeuch.

7 pairs of
black boots

Big E doesn't care for flashy
footwear, but Kofi does! See
page 149!

2 pairs of boots with curly tips

It's important to look for inspiration in unlikely places. Check out Woods' curlicue boots. Last dude who rocked a pair like that in a major way was Iron Sheik back in the day when he was trying to bring death to Hulkamania. Kids used to be terrified of those crazy boots! Now, because of Woods, you see high schoolers riding skateboards while rocking those curlicue joints. Presumably.

The Iron Sheik ✓
@the_ironsheik

[Follow]

XAVIER WOODS YOU STEAL MY BOOTS BUBBA YOU LUCKY I DONT BREAK YOUR ███ ████ NECK YOU OVER WITH ME BUBBA

6:59 PM - 4 Jan 2016

185 Retweets **301** Likes

10   185   301

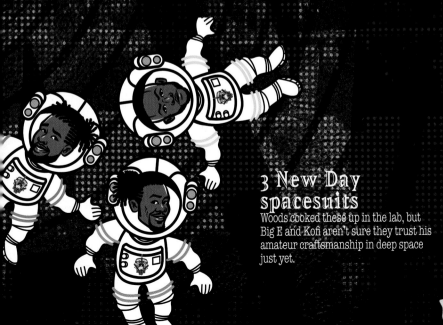

3 New Day spacesuits

Woods cooked these up in the lab, but Big E and Kofi aren't sure they trust his amateur craftsmanship in deep space just yet.

QUIZ TIME:
FINISH THE SENTENCE

1. The New Day began their historic tag team title reign by defeating The Prime Time Players at _____ in 2015.
   A. Hell in a Cell
   B. Battleground
   C. Night of Champions
   D. SummerSlam

2. _____ magazine declared all three New Day members "WWE Wrestler of the Year" in 2015.
   A. The New Yorker
   B. Sports Illustrated
   C. Rolling Stone
   D. Newsweek

3. The lovely bagpipes Xavier played on *SmackDown LIVE* in Glasgow, Scotland, on November 8, 2016 was dubbed _____.
    A. Agnes
    B. Hilda
    C. Morag
    C. Rhona

4. The New Day's record-setting tag team title reign lasted exactly _____ days.
    A. 460
    B. 475
    C. 480
    D. 483

5. _____ is the depraved monster responsible for the untimely demise of Francesca I.
    A. The Miz
    B. Brock Lesnar
    C. Rusev
    D. Chris Jericho

6. The New Day surpassed the team of _____ to become the longest-reigning WWE Tag Team Champions ever.
   A. Team Hell No
   B. The Usos
   C. Paul London and Brian Kendrick
   D. Edge and Christian

7. _____ is the rarely referred to name of The New Day's finishing maneuver.
   A. Midnight Hour
   B. Double Down
   C. Lost in the Woods
   D. Dropzone

8. According to The New Day, _____ is the most intimidating thing about The Wyatt Family.
   A. Vacant stares
   B. Sheep masks
   C. Gene pool
   D. Hygiene

9. The New Day made their in-ring debut as a trio on *SmackDown* on November 28, 2014, by defeating _____.
   A. The Wyatt Family
   B. The Miz, Damien Mizdow & Bad News Barrett
   C. The Shield
   D. Titus O'Neil, Heath Slater, and Curtis Axel

10. All three New Day members were recognized as Tag Team Champions thanks to a ruling named for _____, the WWE Hall of Fame group.
    A. The Four Horsemen
    B. The Freebirds
    C. The Von Erichs
    D. The Road Warriors

As a trio, The New Day are able to compete in WWE as tag team champions thanks to The Freebird Rule, a stipulation allowing any two of three members of a team to defend tag team titles on any given night. In other words, without The Fabulous Freebirds, The New Day might not exist.

Fitting, then, that on the night of April 2, 2016, Big E, Kofi, and Xavier were chosen to induct The Fabulous Freebirds into the WWE Hall of Fame. "It's an honor," Kofi told WWE.com shortly after the ceremony. "It's crazy. It's awesome, though."

The upbeat vibes would continue the following day during *WrestleMania 32*. Big E, Kofi, and Xavier were scheduled to compete against The League of Nations. And while the match proved to be a crowd-pleaser, it was The New Day's entrance that stole the show.

In the weeks preceding *WrestleMania*, the guys had brainstormed several entrance ideas, including arriving in a unicorn-shaped van and flying around atop the horned creatures inside Dallas' AT&T Stadium. Ultimately, it was WWE's Executive Vice President of Talent, Live Events, and Creative, Triple H, who presented Big E, Kofi, and Xavier with an alternate and outrageous concept, one they enthusiastically embraced.

Prior to the trio's match that night, New Day's entrance music filled the stadium and a 20-foot box of Booty-O's cereal sat on the ramp leading to the ring. The towering replica box suddenly tilted to one side and toppled over, spilling giant Booty-O's across the ramp. The frisbee-sized pieces of cereal were quickly followed by Big E, Kofi, and Xavier, who emerged from the massive box dressed in heroic new gear specially made for *WrestleMania*.

The unforgettable entrance had the entire WWE Universe buzzing—and it likely will for years to come.

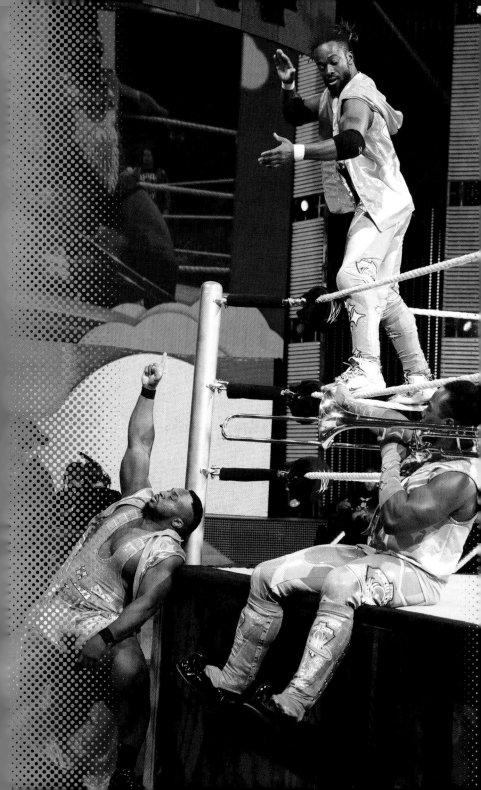

UNICORN HORNS.

Action figures. Boxers. If you can sell it in a store, chances are The New Day's handsome faces have appeared on the product. Check out some of the coolest and most unique merchandise that has been released to celebrate ya boys.

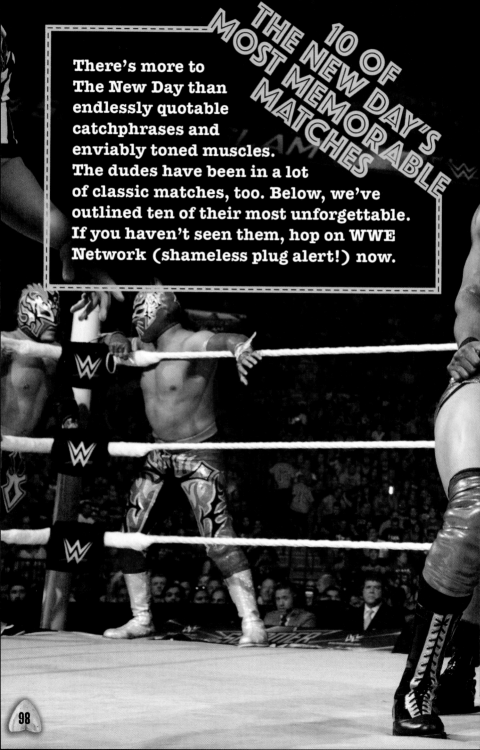

There's more to
The New Day than
endlessly quotable
catchphrases and
enviably toned muscles.
The dudes have been in a lot
of classic matches, too. Below, we've
outlined ten of their most unforgettable.
If you haven't seen them, hop on WWE
Network (shameless plug alert!) now.

The New Day def. The Prime Time Players, The Lucha Dragons, and Los Matadores in a Fatal 4-Way Tag Team Match at SummerSlam 2015

One example of chaos theory states that a butterfly flapping its wings at just the right moment in, say, Santa Ana can alter wind patterns enough to cause a typhoon in Taiwan. In WWE, the same holds true for the power of Kofi Kingston's winged boots. That theory was proven during SummerSlam 2015 when the fleet-footed Superstar, sporting golden, winged footwear, scored a pinfall to usher in New Day's second reign as WWE Tag Team Champions and forever alter the course of WWE history.

The chaos kicked off in Brooklyn on August 23, 2015, when ya boys competed in a Fatal 4-Way Tag Team Match against Los Matadores, The Lucha Dragons, and reigning WWE Tag Team Champions The Prime Time Players. The rules stated that only two competitors could be legal at a time, and the first Superstar to score a pinfall or submission would win the titles for his team. New Day wisely exploited this rule from jump street.

In a cunning gambit, the Dreadlocked Dynamo tagged himself in quickly followed by the other legal man, Big E, attempting to pin him. Before the ploy could work, however, The Prime Time Players' Titus O'Neil frantically broke up the count. Though thwarted, New Day was hardly out of ideas. Later in the bout, Big E and Kofi isolated Darren Young, the other half of the reigning champions, and punished him with a battalion of boot-to-body blows. With Xavier egging him on from ringside, Kofi ascended to the top rope to seal Young's fate. The Prime Time Player, however, countered with an inverted atomic drop before hastily tagging his partner back in.

Recognizing the threat that a steamroller like O'Neil posed, the other competitors converged on him like army ants on apple pie. As might be expected, O'Neil easily disposed of the attackers one by one. With the ring erupting in pandemonium, it became difficult to keep track of the two legal competitors, which gave rise to the idea that earned Kofi his wings.

After O'Neil leveled the other legal competitor in the match, Los Matadores' Fernando, with a Clash of the Titus maneuver, Kofi slyly tagged O'Neil, allowing himself to become the legal man. With help from Big E, the winged warrior then rolled The Prime Time Player from the ring before flying over to a prone Fernando to cover him for the three-count.

The win offered New Day a first taste of what would eventually become a savory 483-day tag team title reign and added another historic chapter to the WWE record books.

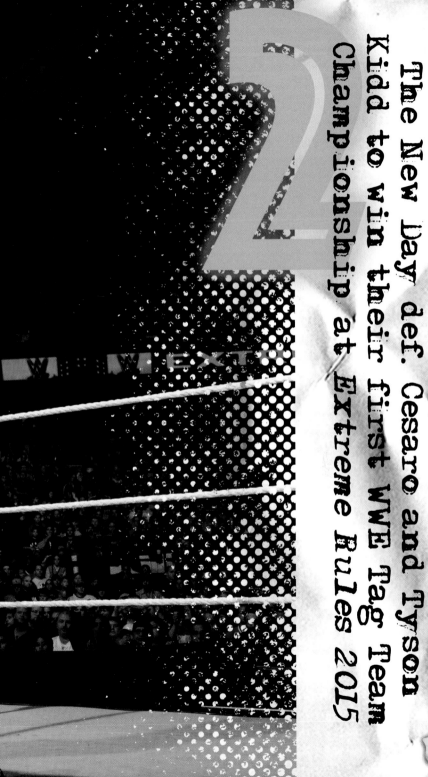

The New Day def. Cesaro and Tyson Kidd to win their first WWE Tag Team Championship at Extreme Rules 2015

The one that started it all. This was the match that validated the sweat and the perseverance, the miles driven and the hours away from home—the grind. Big E, Kofi, and Xavier winning the WWE Tag Team Titles not only forced the WWE Universe and company suits to view New Day through a different lens, it also allowed the trio to exhale a bit, to believe the maverick course they had charted could finally lead to the promised land.

Before ya boys could indulge in either milk or honey, however, they would need to scale a pivotal peak at *Extreme Rules 2015*. At the punishing pay-per-view, WWE Tag Team Champions Cesaro and Tyson Kidd showed no signs of abdicating their position as kings of the mountain any time soon.

On April 26, 2015, New Day nonetheless hoped to dethrone the duo, who had reigned for an impressive 63 days. It would hardly be a coronation, especially in light of the fact that the Swiss Superman and the Hart Dungeon grad had successfully defended their titles against New Day on more than one occasion since becoming champions.

Despite the losses and chants of "New Day sucks!" pelting down on them inside Chicago's Allstate Arena, the trio confidently occupied the squared circle with Big E and Kofi set to compete while Xavier would look on from ringside.

The opening bell ushered in a Kofi vs. Kidd faceoff, which proved to be a fast-paced wrestling clinic. The Canadian's athleticism was on display while Kofi proved adept at countering a series of impressive holds. After the frenetic exchange, the Superstars tagged in their respective partners. The powerhouses squared up until Cesaro ran the ropes, at which point Big E attempted to leap over him. Instead of hurdling Cesaro, however, an unsuspecting Big E found himself jumping into the waiting arms of the Swiss Superman, who promptly slammed him to the canvas.

By the time Big E tagged out, Kofi was buzzing along the apron, itching for action. The Dreadlocked Dynamo quickly went to work punishing a fresh Kidd. Eventually, the worm would turn, and Kingston found himself up against Cesaro, who clobbered his opponent with four uppercuts in the corner.

At one point during the bout, Kofi set up for Trouble in Paradise on Kidd, who countered into a Sharpshooter. Before Kofi would tap, though, he managed to escape the hold. Unfortunately for him, it was out of the shooter and into the spin cycle when the Swiss Superman seized him for a Cesaro Swing.

As Cesaro pinned Kofi, Xavier protested from the apron, distracting the referee. In the ensuing commotion, Kofi would eventually roll up Cesaro and, with a handful of tights, keep the Swiss Superman down for the winning three-count.

The victory would result in a 49-day run with the WWE Tag Team Titles. But even that respectable reign was but a prelude to The New Day's titanic tenure yet to come.

The New Day def. The Usos and Lucha Dragons in a Triple Threat WWE Championship Ladder Match at WWE TLC: *Tables, Ladders & Chairs 2015*

If you were still sleeping on The New Day in December 2015, chances are this match woke you up.

Kicking off *WWE TLC: Tables, Ladders & Chairs*—WWE's yearly demolition derby that inevitably ends with half the roster covered in ice packs and picking splinters out of their butts—The New Day put their Tag Team Titles up for grabs against the dynamic Lucha Dragons and the dangerous Usos.

With Xavier Woods rooting them on from the commentary table, Big E and Kofi Kingston put in that work to ensure their historic title reign did not come to an early end. That includes Big E, who found himself precariously placed underneath a ladder while both Kalisto and Sin Cara climbed toward the titles, picking up the whole structure with one arm and tipping it over. That's not strong. That's scary strong.

This match was less about glorious moments like that, however, and more about just merely surviving. Big E and Kofi fought back through every ladder smash and dizzying fall to stay in the game. At one point, Big E was laid out on the arena floor. Jimmy Uso put a ladder on top of him, then jumped from the turnbuckle in the ring onto E on the outside. It was madness.

In the end, though, it was about picking your spot. With everyone down on the floor, Kalisto began a slow climb up the ladder in the ring. This brought Woods up from the commentary table where he then grabbed Francesca and hurled it at Kalisto, smashing him in the back. This allowed Kingston to send Kalisto off the ladder, then climb it himself to snatch the championships for his side.

Underhanded? Maybe just a little. But sometimes that's what it takes to stay on top.

The New Day def. The Usos for the SmackDown Tag Team Championship at *WWE Battleground 2017*

Batman has The Joker. The Yankees have the Red Sox. And Kanye West has... well, just about everyone. In every worthy endeavor, there exist rivalries in which both sides push the other to elevate their game. In the summer of 2017, it was The Usos who forced New Day to do just that.

Jimmy and Jey Uso vehemently rejected the power of positivity, choosing instead to offer a brooding yin to New Day's upbeat yang. The dynamic was never more evident than at *WWE Battleground*. It was there that Kofi and Xavier, sporting brightly colored Stars-and-Stripes ring gear, would face off against the *SmackDown* Tag Team Champions, who fittingly wore black T-shirts and camouflage pants.

As Big E eagerly looked on from outside the ring, Kofi and Xavier initially appeared as in-sync as ever. Early in the bout, Kofi stunned Jey with a splash before quickly sliding out of the way to allow X-Man to fly off the top rope and drop a punishing elbow across his opponent's chest.

Then it was The Usos' turn. The duo focused their wrath on Xavier, who found himself on the business end of a litany of swift kicks, punishing punches, and bodyslams at the hands of both brothers.

Later in the bout, the Dreadlocked Dynamo would force both Usos outside the ring. His momentum, however, would grind to a halt when he ascended to the top turnbuckle and hurled himself onto the two. Unfortunately for Kofi, The Brothers Uce caught him in mid-air and powerbombed him onto the arena's unforgiving floor.

To avenge his partner, Xavier attempted to ambush his opponents from the top rope only to suffer a stiff uppercut upon landing. Later, as Jimmy prepared to slam X-Man face-first onto the mat, Xavier remarkably reversed the move and instead gave the Samoan his own taste of canvas.

All four Superstars then had to endure a heartstopping series of near pinfalls, each kicking out at the last possible second to prolong their team's chances. Notably, Jey crushed Kofi with a Samoan Splash from the top turnbuckle only to have the Dreadlocked Dynamo magically slip out at the count of two like Houdini from handcuffs.

In the end, though, it would be Xavier who, after refusing to tap out during a submission hold, would finally turn the tables. He once again took to the skies, sailing from the top rope and landing an elbow onto Jimmy's chest. This time, the punishment proved too much as X-Man refused to be thrown until the referee slapped the mat for three.

The win not only gave New Day a much-needed victory over two of their fiercest foes, it also earned them their inaugural run as *SmackDown* Tag Team Champions.

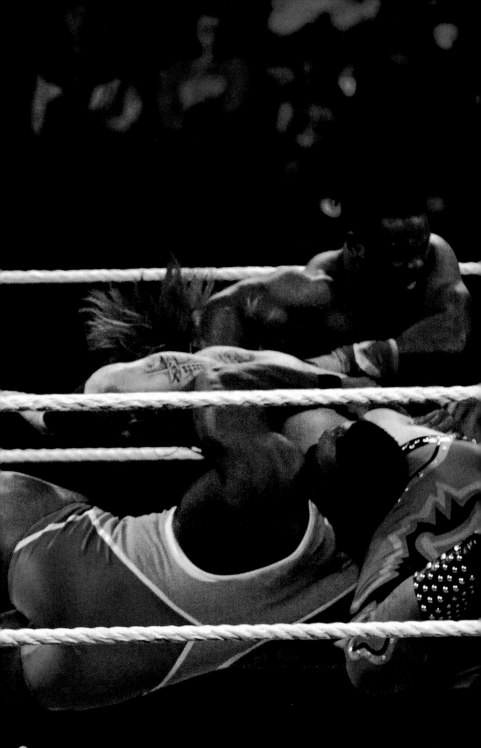

The New Day def. Curtis Axel, Heath Slater, and Titus O'Neil on the November 28, 2014, episode of *SmackDown*

Long before the unicorn horns and trombones, the rainbows and Booty-Os, Big E, Kofi Kingston, and Xavier Woods were just three guys hustling to make a name for themselves in a crowded field and to secure their spot on the WWE roster.

And as the saying goes, you gotta start somewhere. For The New Day, that somewhere was on *SmackDown*, where they would make their team debut against Curtis Axel, Heath Slater, and Titus O'Neil. The bout offered a peek at what would eventually become a global phenomenon as well as the longest-reigning tag team in WWE history.

The initial introduction, however, proved less than auspicious. Despite their enthusiastic entrance, New Day was greeted with a resounding shrug by the notoriously fickle WWE Universe, who weren't about to cough up praise without performance.

Xavier was the first member to represent New Day in the match, squaring off against Axel. The trio's teamwork shone within the first two minutes of the bout when Big E lifted X-Man above a lying Axel and brought him down hard on their opponent.

Xavier would pay, however, when he was trapped in a corner and suffered boots and backbreakers from all three of New Day's rivals. When X-Man finally tagged in Kofi, his partner was prepped and punished Slater with a flying crossbody. Big E then put the screws to Axel with a belly-to-belly suplex that sent him outside the ring, followed quickly by his teammates. This was the moment New Day genuinely began to coalesce. Recognizing an opportunity, Big E set up in the ring and hoisted a running Kofi over the top rope to come crashing down on their foes. The crowd reacted with appreciation and applause. As Big E waited to be fed, Kofi rolled a dazed Slater under the bottom rope. After the big man lifted Slater onto his shoulder, Xavier sailed off the top rope and came crashing down on Slater to set up an easy three-count.

Afterward, the jubilant threesome celebrated as if they'd won the main event at *WrestleMania*. They had no way of knowing at that point they would go on to host WWE's grandest spectacle less than three years later or emerge as the longest-reigning tag team in WWE history. But in such a triumphant and genuine moment, none of that would matter just yet.

The New Day def. AJ Styles and Chris Jericho on the March 7, 2016, episode of Monday Night Raw

What happens when arguably the best wrestler on the planet today and the GOAT himself face off against The New Day? They get schooled, that's what.

AJ Styles and Chris Jericho—known as Y2AJ during their brief, ill-fated partnership—received a *Raw* Tag Team Title opportunity against Big E and Kofi Kingston on the March 7, 2016, edition of Raw, and came scary close to upending the champs.

Styles, who was only two months into his WWE run, kept The New Day on their toes with his sensational offense, including a springboard moonsault that ended in a reverse DDT and a 450 splash. And Jericho, perhaps the craftiest player in the game, seemed to be two steps ahead of the team the entire time.

Yet, despite what the movies try to tell ya, brawn usually outdoes brains. In the final moments of the match, Big E and Jericho traded reversals like comedians trading insults at a roast. The key exchange, however, was won by your boy Big E as Jericho attempted his patented Codebreaker only to be caught in midair. Then, in a tremendous show of his unbelievable strength, E tossed Jericho onto his shoulder and hit the Big Ending for the victory.

The loss was so damaging for Jericho that he attacked Styles after the bell and demolished him with three Codebreakers. Bad news for Y2AJ fans, but good news for The New Day, who dispatched yet another rival team.

Curtis Axel and Ryback def. The New Day on the July 21, 2014, episode of Monday Night Raw

Despite the outcome, this match proved to be a seminal moment in the birth of The New Day. Seeing it and its subsequent promo by Xavier feels a little like watching The Beatles play The Cavern Club in 1962. The magic that would propel them to global stardom is barely distinguishable. But it's there. Bubbling just under the surface. Waiting to burst forth like a soda can that's been shaken in a paint mixer.

At first blush, though, Kofi and Big E look like beta versions of the exuberant New Day cohorts they would eventually become. Dressed in mismatched ring gear, the pair initially exude all the chemistry of a blind date at a funeral home. They're just partners at this point, not yet brothers.

Early in the match, a monstrous Ryback appeared to be manhandling Big E with suplexes—both German and non—and a series of crippling forearms to the back. While Big E struggled to his feet, the crowd ramped up Ryback's signature chant: "Feed me more!" This was usually an indication that the leviathon was poised to level an opponent with a running lariat, but to Big E's credit, he collided with Ryback mid-ring and grounded him with a running clothesline of his own.

The two bewildered bulldozers then slowly found their footing. Before Ryback could retreat to his corner, Big E tagged in his teammate, who wasted no time. Kofi bounced off the top rope with a flying clothesline, stunned Ryback with a dropkick, and finally went for the cover in the wake of a feverish S.O.S. maneuver. After a two-count, Axel dove in to rescue the match. As a result, Big E stormed the ring and took Axel with him over the top rope, leaving the Dreadlocked Dynamo to finish what he had started. Kofi again took to the skies, striking Ryback with a flying crossbody. The move's momentum, however, allowed Ryback to roll through and pin Kofi for the three-count. The defeat left Kofi and Big E demoralized and wondering how things could have gone so wrong. It was Xavier who would finally enlighten them.

Sporting a white suit, white tie, red button-down shirt and whip-smart glasses, the Ph.D. candidate confronted the downtrodden duo. "You cannot move ahead by always doing what you're told," he said as he stood in the ring with them. "Now, this is our time. This is our place . . . We do not ask any longer. Now, we take."

The lesson clearly resonated with Kofi and Big E, and the trio would regroup, revamp, and re-emerge months later on the long and winding road to finally becoming The New Day.

8

The New Day def. Luke Gallows and Karl Anderson on the September 26, 2016, episode of Monday Night Raw

Nine stitches to the forehead. Apparently, that's the price to pay for retaining the WWE Tag Team Championship. Just ask Kofi Kingston.

One night after successfully defending their titles against the team of Luke Gallows and Karl Anderson at *Clash of Champions*, Big E, Kofi, and Xavier were forced to face the good brothers yet again the following night during the September 26, 2016, episode of *Monday Night Raw*.

It didn't help that Gallows and Anderson appeared in a foul mood. The pair were still steamed about the trombone attack that cost them the titles some twenty-four hours earlier. And it showed.

The duo gleefully trained their ire on Kofi, pummeling the athletically adroit Superstar nearly into submission with a buffet of wallops. Before the Dreadlocked Dynamo would cave, though, New Day's infectious energy emerged, and the team rallied to hit The Midnight Hour on Anderson.

Fortunately for the good brother, his partner broke up the count at two-and-a-half. Not only that, the bald bruisers then went on to stagger Big E with a Magic Killer. The bout's back-and-forth, hold-your-breath, did-that-really-just-happen? action refused to relent, leaving the audience on the precipice of palpitations.

With his heavyweight partner hobbled, Kofi reached in for a critical tag, a rivulet of crimson meandering down the Dazed Dynamo's busted-open forehead (the laceration likely occurred when Gallows hurled him into the steel steps earlier in the bout). The blood-speckled canvas resembled something from a grisly Jackson Pollock painting as the wounded Kofi somehow managed to spike Anderson with Trouble in Paradise and crawl atop him for the win.

Victory came at a steep price, to be sure, but it also allowed New Day's championship odometer to roll over to 401 days—and counting.

The New Day def. Enzo Amore and Big Cass, Luke Gallows and Karl Anderson, and The Vaudevillains at *Money in the Bank 2016*

9

With four teams competing for the WWE Tag Team Championship at *Money in the Bank 2016*, the chances of New Day pulling off a win stood at a measly 25 percent. Being that the event took place in Las Vegas, however, Big E, Kofi, and Xavier were eager to prove that sometimes three-of-a-kind actually can beat a full house.

The trio began dealing out insults before the night's Fatal 4-Way Match had even kicked off. A confident New Day had no problem calling out each of the opposing squads: Enzo Amore and Big Cass were no more than a "brokedown Han Solo and a hairless Chewbacca," The Vaudevillains, Aiden English and Simon Gotch, looked like a couple of "Monopoly Men," and Luke Gallows and Karl Anderson were about to be shipped back to Japan.

Then chaos. After the opening bell, Big E and Kofi sized up the six other competitors crowding the ring alongside them until a flurry of punches and clotheslines all around sent half the Superstars over the top rope and crashing onto the arena floor.

Early in the bout, Amore and Cass nearly broke the bank with a Rocket Launcher to Anderson, who was saved by his Club comrade Gallows thanks to the match's no-disqualification stipulation.

Gallows played pit boss once again moments later, breaking up a second pin after The Vaudevillains struck Kofi with a Whirling Dervish. The 6-foot-8, 290-pound Gallows then went on offense. He and Anderson punished English with their Magic Killer, but this time it was Big E's turn to disrupt the pin.

The big man then muscled Anderson onto his shoulder in preparation for a Big Ending. Before he could, though, Cass leveled the vulnerable Club crony with a big boot. Seizing the opportunity, New Day bet it all on Midnight Hour, allowing Kofi to cover a ragdolled Anderson for the pinfall.

With that, New Day's 301-day title reign remained alive and kicking. It also showed opponents that no matter what cards ya boys are dealt, they can always be counted on to go all-in on every match.

10

New Day def. The Lucha Dragons and
Neville on the February 22, 2016,
episode of Monday Night Raw

This match made the list for two reasons: 1) It's that rare instance of all three members of New Day competing without having to invoke the Freebird Rule, and 2) Facing off against skilled highflyers like Neville, Kalisto, and Sin Cara is akin to fending off a squadron of fighter jets with your bare hands.

Early in the Six-Man Tag Team Match, things took a daunting turn for New Day when Xavier was tossed from the ring and clipped his head on the adjacent steel steps. Rather than forgo the match, Big E scrambled to help his dazed teammate and rolled him back onto the canvas, where he somehow managed to tag in Kofi.

For his part, Neville was finally able to muster enough speed to tag in Sin Cara, who unleashed another wave of his team's aerial assault. After enduring the impact of both a flying crossbody and a leap through the ropes onto the floor, Kofi was nearly done in when Sin Cara dragged him back into the ring and nailed a backflip off the second rope directly onto him. Fortunately for Kofi, Big E rushed in to break the count. The big man's heroics cost him, though, as he was met with a springboard dropkick by Kalisto.

New Day's opponents really could have used an air traffic controller by the time Neville landed a 450 Splash onto Big E, who lay prone outside the ring. The frenetic scene didn't end there as Kalisto used Neville's back as a springboard to jump off and divebomb a 450 Splash of his own onto Xavier.

Back in the ring, Sin Cara ascended to the top turnbuckle to drop a senton bomb onto the legal man, Kofi. When Kofi dodged the missile, Sin Cara was able to hoist the New Day veteran atop his shoulders. But before the luchador could execute another maneuver, Kofi began tugging at his mask. The confusion allowed Kofi just enough time to execute Trouble in Paradise and ground Sin Cara for the win.

The match shone a spotlight on Big E, Kofi, and Xavier for their determination, cohesiveness, and willingness to do whatever it takes to win. The victory may not have been pretty, but we never said New Day was *all* rainbows and unicorns.

THE NEW DAY HOST WRESTLEMANIA 33

After The New Day's monumental entrance at *WrestleMania 32*, the question looming over the trio was "How can we possibly top ourselves next year on The Grandest Stage of Them All?" But leave it to the three-man thrill ride to eclipse even a colossal, 20-foot-tall box of Booty-Os.

On February 20, 2017, it was announced that Big E, Kofi, and Xavier would serve as hosts of *WrestleMania 33*. That revelation meant that New Day, who were nearly a disappointing footnote in the history of WWE, would join the ranks of The Rock in playing Masters of Ceremony for sports entertainment's most prestigious event.

Amid soaring expectations, the trio managed to pull off what many consider to be one of the most entertaining shows in *WrestleMania* history. The festive fuse was lit on April 2, 2017, with Big E's booming baritone: "Orlando, don't you dare be sour!" he implored the 75,245 attendees inside Florida's Camping World Stadium. "Clap for your *WrestleMania* hosts, and feel the power!"

The trio then entered wearing ring gear inspired by the video game *Final Fantasy* as Kofi pushed a New Day Pops ice cream cart. The entrance felt joyous, electrifying, and surreal all at the same time, befitting the outrageous spectacle about to commence.

New Day kept the over-the-top action chugging along throughout, announcing the return of fan favorites Matt and Jeff Hardy moments before the night's Fatal 4-Way Tag Team Ladder Match for the WWE Raw Tag Team Championship. The trio also oversaw a brutal match between Goldberg and Brock Lesnar, a touching marriage proposal featuring John Cena and Nikki Bella, and what would prove to be the legendary Undertaker's final bout.

In the end, The New Day's performance would receive wide praise. *Rolling Stone* magazine weighed in, saying Big E, Kofi, and Xavier "were excellent hosts; funny when called upon and out of the way when not." The show clearly demonstrated the trio's ability to entertain and provided yet another feather in their collective cap.

FINAL FANTASY BECOMES A REALITY

If you're not much of a gamer, you may have wondered why The New Day were outfitted like renaissance faire swashbucklers at *WrestleMania 33*. The boys were paying tribute to characters in the video game *Final Fantasy XIV*, specifically in the Stormblood expansion pack.

Woods' gauntlets and shin guards of the Monk are in tribute to the game's Monk class

Big E's robe and katana are based on the Samurai in the game

The Red Mage in *FF XIV* inspired Kofi's boots and rapier

143

QUIZ TIME: TAG TEAM HISTORY

WE KNOW YOU LOVE THE NEW DAY MORE THAN ANY TAG TEAM IN RECORDED HUMAN HISTORY, SO MUCH SO THAT YOU BLEED NEW DAY BLUE...OR WHATEVER COLOR YA BOYS ARE SPORTING ON A GIVEN NIGHT. THAT SAID, IT IS STILL ESSENTIAL TO BE A STUDENT OF THE GAME, AND WE DON'T MEAN TRIPLE H (UNLESS YOU ARE CURRENTLY TRAINING IN NXT). THE NEW DAY DID NOT BECOME A REVOLUTIONARY SQUAD WITHOUT STUDYING THE PIONEERS THAT CAME BEFORE THEM. YOU SHOULD DO THE SAME. SPEND A REASONABLE AMOUNT OF TIME BINGE-WATCHING VINTAGE TAG TEAM MATCHES ON THE WWE NETWORK. ABOUT EIGHTEEN TO TWENTY HOURS PER DAY WILL DO. YOUR FAMILY WILL UNDERSTAND. THEN HIT THE BELOW QUESTIONS TO SEE HOW MUCH YOU LEARNED.

1. Before The New Day came along, Demolition boasted the longest tag team championship reign in WWE history. Which team was responsible for defeating Demolition and ending their 478-day reign in July of 1989?

    A. Mr Fuji and Mr Saito

    B. Andre the Giant and Haku

    C. The Hart Foundation

    D. The Brain Busters

2. Was the Honky Tonk Man's guitar the great, great uncle of Francesca? We think so. What musically inspired tag team did Honky Tonk Man form with Greg "The Hammer" Valentine in 1988?

    A. Shake, Rattle & Roll

    B. Guns & Roses

    C. Rhythm & Blues

    D. Starsky & Hutch

3. All three members of The New Day have college degrees, but they never graduated from anger management school live on *Raw* like these hot-tempered former tag champs.

    A. Sheamus and Cesaro

    B. Team Hell No

    C. Team Rhodes Scholars

    D. The New Age Outlaws

4. One glance through this book is irrefutable proof that the camera loves The New Day…perhaps as much as this Attitude Era duo who invented the five-second pose "for the benefit of those with flash photography."

    A. Edge and Christian

    B. The Hardy Boyz

    C. The Dudley Boyz

    D. The APA

5. The lineage of the current *Raw* Tag Team Championships traces back to 2002 when they were introduced as the WWE Tag Team Championships and made exclusive to *SmackDown*. Weird, right? Which of New Day's future bosses was responsible for introducing them?
   A. Daniel Bryan
   B. Shane McMahon
   C. Stephanie McMahon
   D. Vince McMahon

6. Which pairing holds the distinction of having the shortest tag team championship reign of all time, clocking in at five minutes long, or a mere 482 days, 23 hours and 55 minutes short of The New Day's mark?
   A. Powers of Pain
   B. Beauty and the Man Beast
   C. 3-Minute Warning
   D. The Miz and John Cena

7. When Xavier Woods rocked curly-toed boots in the ring, many believed he was channeling the fashion sense of another tag team champion, Iron Sheik. Which fellow WWE Hall of Famer joined the Sheik to claim the gold?
   A. Abdullah the Butcher
   B. William "The Refrigerator" Perry
   C. Sgt. Slaughter
   D. Nikolai Volkoff

8. If you root for The Usos in a match against The New Day, you might be booty...unless you are their dad. In that case, you have a very famous booty and a WWE Tag Team Championship reign with Scotty 2 Hotty. To the WWE Universe, you are beloved Hall of Famer _____.
   A. Rikishi
   B. Razor Ramon
   C. Kurt Angle
   D. Ron Simmons

9. To maintain success in WWE, you must always stay one step ahead of the competition. You can bet The New Day has been scouting up-and-comers such as the Authors of Pain, whose manager guided arguably the most dominant team in sports entertainment history, known as _____.
   A. The Dudley Boyz
   B. The Shield
   C. The Nexus
   D. The Road Warriors

10. Speaking of managers, The New Day has never needed one. But if they did, we bet it would be this legend, whose infamous megaphone would harmonize nicely with the smooth sounds of Francesca II: Turbo.
    A. Captain Lou Albano
    B. Jimmy Hart
    C. Bobby "The Brain" Heenan
    D. Slick

Answers: 1.D, 2.C, 3.B, 4.A, 5.C, 6.D, 7.D, 8.A, 9.D, 10.B

KOFI'S TOP 10 COOLEST PAIRS OF KICKS

s it the shoes? Well, nah. Kofi Kingston s an insane athlete. He could be wearing a pair of orange Crocs and still pull off the craziest moves imaginable. But when the man puts on a pair of fresh sneakers and takes off from the top rope, damn does he ook good flying through the air. Here, Kofi shares the ten pairs of shoes that made him the man with the best-dressed feet in WWE.

A
The shoe: Under Armour Curry Two Low "Chef"
The night: *Raw*, June 13, 2016

B
The shoe: Nike Lebron 12 "Finish Your Breakfast"
The night: *Raw*, May 12, 2016

C
The shoe: Nike Kyrie 2 "Neon Green, Glow in the
Dark Ice Cream" Mache Custom
The night: *Raw*, May 3, 2017

D
The shoe: Jeremy Scott Adidas Dark Knight Wings 3.0
The night: *WrestleMania 32*

E
The shoe: Nike Zoom Hyperflight Tiger
The night: *WWE Main Event*, August 21, 2013

F
The shoe: Jeremy Scott Adidas Shark Fin
The night: *Raw*, November 2, 2015

G
The shoe: Jeremy Scott Adidas Wings 2.0 "Splatter Paint" Mache Custom
The night: *WrestleMania 33*

H
The shoe: Nike Lebron 9 "Miami Hurricanes"
The night: *WWE Battleground; Raw*, June 21, 2014
(Kofi note: This was the first time The New Day
appeared as a collective on television.)

I
The shoe: Nike Zoom LeBron Soldier 10 "Unicorn" Mache Custom
The night: *SummerSlam 2016*

J
The shoe: Jeremy Scott
Adidas Wings 3.0 Gold
The night: *SummerSlam 2015*

STORY TIME: FILL IN THE BLANKS

One morning, Big E, Kofi, and Xavier were riding in their

_____(adjective) car to *Monday Night Raw*, but first they needed to fill their tank with

_____(noun). They pulled into the first _____(noun) station they could find. Since Big E was _____-ing (verb) along with the radio, Kofi got out to _____ (verb) the gas. _____(exclamation), Big E shouted to Xavier, who was _____-ing (verb) in the backseat. X-Man woke up and

_____-ed (verb) to the store so he could buy a bag of _____ (adjective) chips. Once inside, the clerk gave him a _____ (adjective) look. Xavier had forgotten to take off his unicorn _____(noun). When he went to pay, though, the clerk was also wearing a _____(noun) horn. The two shook

_____(plural noun) and Xavier

walked out and climbed into the backseat of the

_____(noun). From there, Big E

cranked up the _____(noun) and

the three hit the _____(noun) again.

Then the _____(adjective) car

began to sputter and _____(verb)

and Big E had to _____(verb) off the

road. The three parked the broken-down car directly

in front of a _____(noun) ranch.

With only an hour to get to the arena, Kofi asked

the rancher if they could borrow three

_____(plural noun).

After the _____

(adjective) rancher agreed, The

New Day saddled up and began to

_____(verb)

to *Raw*. Not only did the trio

make it on time, they even

won their match against

the _____

(adjective) and powerful tag team

of _____(person's

name) and _____

(person's name). New Day rocks!

OUTSIDE THE ROPES WITH BIG E

What are your favorite sports teams?

The Iowa Hawkeyes. "The Word is Fight! Fight! Fight for IOWA . . ."

Do you have any pets?

Nope, but when I was a kid I had two gerbils named Midnight (all black) and Oreo (black and white). Imaginative, I know. . . .

Did you have any nicknames growing up?

Big E. Everyone butchered my government name and I've been barrel-chested for as long as I can remember. Also, Waffles. My college teammate Kenny Iwebema coined the term. He claimed I would just "hangrily" run into apartments screaming, "WAFFLES!!"

What was your favorite school subject?

English. I had several great English teachers but Mrs. Adams with the untamed gray hair, soothing voice, and adoration for Enya really spurred my interest in reading and writing.

Whom did you idolize growing up?

Derrick Brooks. The man is a Hall of Fame linebacker but a better human being. The Walter Payton Man of the Year regularly took underprivileged kids to South Africa among a myriad of other charitable acts.

Do you have any weird pet peeves?

The term "pet peeve." Am I a grandmother in a sewing circle? Do I wave my fist from my porch at passersby who dare step on my gardenias? Why isn't there a more contemporary-sounding phrase to describe this sentiment?

Do you have a story about a crazy fan interaction?

Naw, just a lot of people aggressively shaking their hips at us. But that's the norm.

BREAK IT DOWN LIKE BIG E

Rhythm. Some say you're either born with it or you're not. But trust and believe, it's in you... somewhere. Maybe it's buried behind your embarrassing rendition of "The Nae Nae," or underneath that iffy version of "The Shmoney Dance" you dropped at the club that one time, or maybe it's lying beside that cringe-worthy interpretation of "The Carlton" you busted out at that wedding a few years back. No matter your dance skills, we're confident you'll be able to cut up with the best of 'em after learning "Big E's Hip Swivel Shimmy"™ in ten easy steps.

STEP 1: To begin, place your feet shoulder-width apart, bend at the knees, and allow your arms to rest loosely by your sides.

STEP 2: Gyrate your hips in a circular motion by moving them in the following sequence: forward and to the left.

STEP 3: Keep your hips pointed out to the left while moving your posterior from the forward position to the back, allowing it to stick out behind you.

STEP 4: Keep your posterior stuck out behind you while shifting your hips from left to right.

STEP 5: Keep your hips pointed out to the right while thrusting your pelvis to the front.

STEP 6: To complete the circle, shift your hips from right to left.

STEP 7: Repeat Steps 1 through 6 in a circular motion, continuing to do so throughout the length of the dance.

STEP 8: While gyrating, bend your right elbow until your forearm is parallel to the floor.

STEP 9: Repeat the previous step using your left arm. Alternate these movements between the right and left arm as if running in place.

STEP 10: Combine the previous nine steps into one fluid motion. And be sure to smile!

Congratulations, you've mastered "Big E's Hip Swivel Shimmy."™

Now quick, go hit the dance floor, fool!

QUIZ TIME: FINAL EXAM

SO YOU ACED THOSE WARM-UP QUESTIONS BACK ON PAGES 30, 64, 88, AND 144 AND NOW YOU FANCY YOURSELF A BEACON OF POSITIVITY? THINK AGAIN, SON! LIKE A QUICK SET OF HINDU SQUATS BEFORE YOUR MUSIC HITS, THAT WAS JUST A WARMUP! NOW COMES THE REAL CHALLENGE. DELIVER A MENTAL UNICORN STOMP TO THE QUESTIONS BELOW. ANSWER ALL TEN CORRECTLY (OK NINE, NOBODY'S PERFECT) AND THEN YOU HAVE BECOME TRULY ENLIGHTENED.

USE OF THE INTERNET, WWE NETWORK, OR THE NEW DAY-LOREAN TIME MACHINE IS STRICTLY PROHIBITED AND TRUST US, WE'LL FIND OUT!

1. Which of the following made The New Day queasy about celebrating their one-year anniversary in Nashville?
   A. The Tennessee Titans
   B. Country music
   C. Too close to Knoxville, where Kane lives
   D. Connie Britton

2. Which of the below teams did not join New Day on Team Raw to battle SmackDown in a Survivor Series Tag Team Elimination Match at *Survivor Series 2016?*

    A. The Ascension

    B. Cesaro and Sheamus

    C. Enzo and Big Cass

    D. The Shining Stars

    E. Luke Gallows and Karl Anderson

3. Following the 2017 Superstar Shake-up, what team did the New Day interrupt and call out on their *SmackDown Live* debut?

    A. Breezango

    B. The Colons

    C. Strike Force

    D. The Usos

4. For what university did Big E play as a defensive tackle on the football team from 2004–2006?

    A. Notre Dame

    B. Iowa

    C. Michigan State

    D. Oklahoma

5. Which team did The New Day defeat at *Roadblock* in March 2016, on the same momentous night the trio unveiled Booty-O's cereal?
    A. The Usos
    B. The Lucha Dragons
    C. The Wyatt Family
    D. King Barrett and Sheamus

6. Which New Day member went one-on-one with "The Beast" Brock Lesnar at a special *WWE Live* event in Tokyo, Japan?
    A. Big E
    B. Kofi Kingston
    C. Xavier Woods
    D. Francesca

7. At which 2015 event did the New Day fend off the Dudley Boyz to retain their WWE Tag Team Titles by smacking Bubba Ray with a broken trombone?
    A. Tables, Ladders & Chairs
    B. Hell in a Cell
    C. Backlash
    D. Money in the Bank

8. Who saved Kofi from elimination in the *2016 Royal Rumble* and helped him swipe some popcorn from fans at ringside?

    A. Big E

    B. Rusev

    C. The Rosebuds

    D. JBL

9. Which of the below was not one of the teams The New Day defeated in a Fatal Four Way Match at Money in the Bank 2016?

    A. Big Cass and Enzo Amore

    B. The Club

    C. The Vaudevillains

    D. The Social Outcasts

10. On which comedy series did New Day make an appearance in 2017?

    A. *Modern Family*

    B. *Adam Ruins Everything*

    C. *Brooklyn Nine-Nine*

    D. *The Goldbergs*

Answers: 1.B, 2.A, 3.D, 4.B, 5.D, 6.B, 7.B, 8.A, 9.D, 10.B

THE OFFICIAL NEW DAY GLOSSARY OF TERMS

Puft! Fibbledybops! Krimsters! Wait. Are any of those even words? Who knows? Here's the thing, they could be. 'Cause when you keep it as tight as The New Day, you can make up your own vocab. Who in their right mind is gonna tell you otherwise? Merriam? Webster? Please. You wanna make up an entire language that only you and your squad can understand? Get on that. Until then, feel free to roll with The New Day's vernacular, some of which they've graciously shared below.

Brolic | adjective
There's big, there's buff, and then there's brolic. The term is said to derive from the *Dragon Ball Z* character Broly. Look it up in the dictionary and you'd see a picture of Big E next to it.
See also: CT Fletcher, Kimbo Slice, Deebo from *Friday*.

Bayyybeeee | noun
Added onto the end of a sentence or thought as the ultimate emphasis. An exclamation point's exclamation point.

Challónge | noun
When one makes a claim that is assumed to be completely outrageous, one may yell, "CHALLÓNGE!" in hopes to call out the individual publicly, or instigate the situation to which that person has made his statement. Pronounced with the same delivery given by the tap-dancing legend Howard "Sandman" Sims.
See also: *The Cosby Show*, Season 6, Episode 19.

Four fingers and a thumb | noun
An accusatory way to point at someone. The age-old saying goes, "When you point a finger, remember you are pointing three more back at yourself!" Well, when we point at someone, we point all fingers at that person. We also point the thumb for extra emphasis. We leave NO DOUBT that any blame would fall upon on us. We also make sure to raise the arm high above the accused and tilt the hand downward from the wrist, because the scolding is more emphatic and condescending when it comes from above. If the situation calls for it, the hand can be slightly angled to the outside for extra degradation. Usually goes hand-in-hand (pun intended) with a well-timed "Gatcho ass!"

Gatcho ass | verb
Pronounced "Gatcho ass!" (short for "got your ass!"). When one has prevailed in a verbal, physical, or psychological joust, they let the loser know that they have been got. Checkmate. Domino. There are many styles in which this news can be delivered: With malice, arrogance, or a foreign accent, to name a few.

Jawn | noun
We use it in reference to an attractive woman. In Philadelphia, they use it in reference to literally everything. Like you might hear someone in Philly say, "Did you get that jawn down at the jawn?"

The Lab | noun
A place where one goes to improve their skills, specifically in the gaming world. When one wants to tinker with and improve the elements of their game, one should go to The Lab.

Molly-whop | verb
To break your foot off in one's hindquarters; to lambast.

Roughneck | noun
Popularized by MC Lyte's 1993 hit single, "Ruff Neck," which describes its central character as "a dude with an attitude / Only needs his fingers with his food / Karl Kani saggin' timbos draggin' / Frontin' in his ride with his home boys braggin'."

Shhhuh! | verb
An expression emoting disbelief and/or disgust with a statement or situation. Pronounced rapidly, usually high-pitched; sounding like "shhh" but with a quick tightening of the abdominal region and slight shrugging of both shoulders.

Tender vittles | noun
A good meal. Edible sustenance.
See also: vittles

That WORK! | noun
The act of getting worked over, or beaten very badly. One might say something along the lines of, "If you want to challenge me, you're more than welcome to come and get that WORK!" When one is able to do this with complete and utter ease, it is known as "light work."

WORD UP

Just as The New Day eventually found its groove, it's up to you to find the following words that have helped to make the group such a success.

A	B	U	N	I	C	O	R	N	W	X	A	V	K
U	C	B	L	Y	Y	Y	T	O	O	T	O	O	O
U	W	B	O	O	T	Y	O	S	M	M	N	R	F
P	O	E	V	L	T	G	A	A	W	G	W	C	I
U	N	Y	F	R	A	N	C	E	S	C	A	N	E
P	J	A	L	W	A	S	V	X	U	Q	T	T	E
D	C	A	E	L	V	D	B	D	Q	P	X	R	U
O	X	T	V	L	W	R	I	E	D	O	X	O	N
W	W	Y	O	I	O	B	G	P	A	S	Y	M	I
N	O	X	Q	V	O	C	E	E	S	I	Y	B	K
D	O	W	Q	D	D	R	Y	U	T	T	Y	O	T
O	J	P	O	P	S	E	G	O	O	I	O	N	R
W	T	N	A	T	T	A	R	A	B	V	O	E	N
N	E	W	D	A	Y	S	C	A	L	E	E	E	C

BIG E

KOFI

WOODS

FRANCESCA

NEW DAY

POPS

POSITIVE

BOOTY-OS

UPUPDOWNDOWN

TROMBONE

UNICORN

ACKNOWLEDGMENTS

The authors of this book would like to extend their deepest gratitude to the esteemed Malcolm Gladwell, without whom *The Book of Booty* would not be possible. He didn't actually have anything to do with the publication, per se, but just knowing he was out there writing books was kind of inspiring.

ABOUT THE AUTHORS

Greg Adkins has worked as a writer and editor at *People* magazine and WWE, and is currently busy traveling, surfing and finishing his third stage play, *Ormond Bee Company*.

Ryan Murphy is the Executive Editorial Director of WWE Digital. He would like to thank his parents for encouraging his writing and sending him to college so he could eventually co-author *The Book of Booty*.